A TALE OF A TUB

Written by
Ben Jonson

2015

Table of Contents

DRAMATIS PERSONÆ - 4 -
PROLOGUE. - 5 -
ACT I - 6 -
SCENE I - 7 -
SCENE II - 12 -
SCENE III - 20 -
SCENE IV - 24 -
ACT II - 29 -
SCENE I - 30 -
ACT III - 55 -
SCENE I - 56 -
SCENE II - 65 -
SCENE III - 71 -
SCENE IV - 74 -
SCENE V - 78 -
ACT IV - 84 -
SCENE I - 85 -
SCENE II - 91 -
SCENE III - 95 -
SCENE IV - 101 -
SCENE V - 107 -
ACT V - 113 -
SCENE I - 114 -
SCENE II - 115 -
SCENE III - 126 -
SCENE IV - 131 -
SCENE V - 133 -
THE EPILOGUE - 139 -

DRAMATIS PERSONÆ

CHANON (Canon) HUGH, *Vicar of Paneras, and* CAPTAIN THUMS.
SQUIRE TUB, *or* TRIPOLY, *of Totten-Court.*
BASKET-HILTS, his Man and Governor.
JUSTICE PREAMBLE, *alias* BRAMBLE, *of Maribone.*
MILES METAPHOR, *his Clerk.*
POL MARTIN, *Huisher to* Lady TUB.
TOBIE TURFE, High Constable of Kentish-Town.
JOHN CLAY, of Kilborn, Tilemaker, the Bridegroom.
IN-AND-IN MEDLAY, of Islington, Cooper and Headborough.
RASI' CLENCH, of Hamstead, Farrier and Petty Constable.
TO-PAN, Tinker, or Metal-Man of Belsise, Thirdborough.
DIOGENES SCRIBEN, of Chalcot, the great Writer.
HANNIBAL (Ball) PUPPY, the High Constable's Man.
FATHER ROSIN, the Minstrel, and his two Boys.
BLACK JACK, Lady TUB'S *Butler.*
LADY TUB, of Totten, the Squire's Mother.
DIDO WISPE, *her Woman.*
SIBIL TURFE, Wife to the High Constable.
AWDREY TURFE, her Daughter, the Bride.
JOAN, JOYCE, MADGE, PARNEL GRISEL, *and* KATE, *Maids of the* Bridal. Servants.
SCENE. — FINSBURY HUNDRED

PROLOGUE.

No state-affairs, nor any politic club,
Pretend we in our Tale, here, of a Tub:
But acts of clowns and constables, to-day
Stuff out the scenes of our ridiculous play.
A cooper's wit, or some such busy spark,
Illumining the high constable, and his clerk,
And all the neighbourhood, from old records,
Of antique proverbs, drawn from Whitson-lords
And their authorities, at Wakes and Ales,
With country precedents, and old wives' tales,
We bring you now, to shew what different things
The cotes of clowns are from the courts of kings.

ACT I

SCENE I

Totten-Court. — Before Lady TUB'S House

Enter Canon HUGH.

Hugh. Now on my faith, old bishop Valentine,
You have brought us nipping weather. — *Februere*
Doth cut and shear — your day and diocese
Are very cold. All your parishioners,
As well your laics as your quiristers,
Had need to keep to their warm feather beds,
If they be sped of loves: this is no season,
To seek new makes in; though sir Hugh of Paneras
Be hither come to Totten, on intelligence,
To the young lord of the manor, 'squire Tripoly,
On such an errand as a mistress is.
What, 'squire! I say. — *[Calls.]* Tub I should call him too;
Sir Peter Tub was his father, a saltpetre-man;
Who left his mother, lady Tub of Totten-
Court, here, to revel, and keep open house in;
With the young 'squire her son, and's governor Basket-
Hilts, both by sword and dagger: *[Calls again.]* Domine
Armiger Tub, 'squire Tripoly! *Expergiscere!*
I dare not call aloud lest she should hear me,
And think I conjured up the spirit, her son,
In priest's lack-Latin: O she is jealous
Of all mankind for him.

Tub. [appears at the window.] Canon, is't you?

Hugh. The vicar of Paneras, 'squire Tub! wa'hoh!

Tub. I come, I stoop unto the call, sir Hugh!

Hugh. He knows my lure is from his love, fair Awdrey,
The high constable's daughter of Kentish-town here, master Tobias Turfe.

Enter TUB in his night-gown.

Tub. What news of him?

Hugh. He has waked me
An hour before I would, sir; and my duty
To the young worship of Totten-Court, 'squire Tripoly!'
Who hath my heart, as I have his: Your mistress
Is to be made away from you this morning,
St. Valentine's day: there are a knot of clowns,
The council of Finsbury, so they are styled,
Met at her father's; all the wise of the hundred;
Old Rasi' Clench of Hamstead, petty constable,
In-and-in Medlay, cooper of Islington,
And headborough; with loud To-Pan, the tinker
Or metal-man of Belsise, the thirdborough;
And D'ogenes Scriben, the great writer of Chalcot.

Tub. And why all these?

Hugh. Sir, to conclude in council,
A husband or a make for mistress Awdrey;
Whom they have named and pricked down, Clay of Kilborn,
A tough young fellow, and a tilemaker.

Tub. And what must he do?

Hugh. Cover her, they say;
And keep her warm, sir: mistress Awdrey Turfe,
Last night did draw him for her Valentine;
Which chance, it hath so taken her father and mother,.
(Because themselves drew so on Valentine's eve
Was thirty year,) as they will have her married
To-day by any means; they have sent a messenger
To Kilborn, post, for Clay; which when I knew,
I posted with the like to worshipful Tripoly,
The 'squire of Totten: and my advice to cross it.

Tub. What is't, sir Hugh?

Hugh. Where is your governor Hilts?
Basket must do it.

Tub. Basket shall be call'd. —
Hilts! can you see to rise? [*Aloud.*

Hilts. [appears at the window.] Cham not blind, sir,
With too much light.

Tub. Open your t'other eye,
And view if it be day.

Hilts. Che can spy that
At's little a hole as another, through a milstone. [*Exit above..*

Tub. He will have the last word, though he talk bilk for't.

Hugh. Bilk! what's that?

Tub. Why, nothing: a word signifying
Nothing; and borrowed here to express nothing.

Hugh. A fine device!

Tub. Yes, till we hear a finer.
What's your device now, canon Hugh?

Hugh. In private,
Lend it your ear; I will not trust the air with it,
Or scarce my shirt; my cassock shall not know it;
If I thought it did I'd burn it.

Tub. That's the way,
You have thought to get a new one, Hugh: is't worth it?
Let's hear it first.

Hugh. Then hearken, and receive it. [*Whispers him*
This 'tis, sir. Do you relish it?

Enter HILTS, *and walks by, making himself ready.*

Tub. If Hilts
Be close enough to carry it; there's all.

Hilts. It is no sand, nor butter-milk: if it be,
Ich'am no zive, or watering-pot, to draw
Knots i' your 'casions. If you trust me, zo;
If not, praform it your zelves. Cham no man's wife,
But resolute Hilts: you'll vind me in the buttry. [*Exit.*

Tub. A testy, but a tender clown as wool,
And melting as the weather in a thaw!
He'll weep you like all April; but he'll roar you
Like middle March afore: he will be as mellow,
And tipsy too, as October; and as grave
And bound up like a frost (with the new year)
In January; as rigid as he is rustic.

Hugh. You know his nature, and describe it well;
I'll leave him to your fashioning.

Tub. Stay, sir Hugh;
Take a good angel with you for your guide;
[Gives him a piece of money.
And let this guard you homeward, as the blessing
To our device. *[Exit.*

Hugh. I thank you, 'squire's worship,
Most humbly — for the next: for this I am sure of.
O for a quire of these voices, now,
To chime in a man's pocket, and cry chink!
One doth not chirp, it makes no harmony.
Grave justice Bramble next must contribute;
His charity must offer at this wedding:
I'll bid more to the bason and the bride-ale,
Although but one can bear away the bride.
I smile to think how like a lottery
These weddings are. Clay hath her in possession,
The 'squire he hopes to circumvent the Tile-kin;
And now, if justice Bramble do come off,
'Tis two to one but Tub may lose his bottom. *[Exit.*

SCENE II

Kentish-Town. — A Room in TURFE'S House.

Enter CLENCH, MEDLAY, D'OGE SCRIBEN, BALL, PUPPY, and PAN.

Clench. Why, it is thirty year, e'en as this day now,
Zin Valentine's day, of all days kursin'd, look you;
And the zamè day o' the month as this Zin Valentine,
Or I am vowly deceived —

Med. That our high constable,
Master Tobias Turfe, and his dame were married:
I think you are right. But what was that Zin Valentine?
Did you ever know 'un, goodman Clench?

Clench. Zin Valentine!
He was a deadly zin, and dwelt at Highgate,
As I have heard; but 'twas avore my time:
He was a cooper too, as you are, Medlay,
An In-and-in: a woundy brag young vellow,
As the 'port went o' hun then, and in those days.

Scri. Did he not write his name Sim Valentine?
Vor I have met no Sin in Finsbury books;
And yet I have writ them six or seven times over.

Pan. O you mun look for the nine deadly Sins,
In the church-books, D'oge: not [in] the high constable's:
Nor in the county's: zure, that same zin Valentine,
He was a stately zin, an' he were a zin,
And kept brave house.

Clench. At the Cock-and-Hen in Highgate.
You have fresh'd my memory well in't, neighbour Pan:
He had a place in last king Harry's time,
Of sorting all the young couples; joining them,
And putting them together; which is yet
Praform'd, as on his day — zin Valentine:
As being the zin of the shire, or the whole county:
I am old Rivet still, and bear a brain,
The Clench, the varrier, and true leach of Hamstead.

Pan. You are a shrew antiquity, neighbour Clench,
And a great guide to all the parishes!
The very bell-weather of the hundred, here,
As I may zay. Master Tobias Turfe,
High constable, would not miss you, for a score on us,
When he do 'scourse of the great charty to us.

Pup. What's that, a horse? can 'scourse nought but a horse,
And that in Smithveld. Charty! I ne'er read o' hun,
In the old Fabian's chronicles; nor I think
In any new: he may be a giant there,
For aught I know.

Scri. You should do well to study
Records, fellow Ball, both law and poetry.

Pup. Why, all's but writing and reading, is it, Scriben?
An it be any more, it is mere cheating zure,
Vlat cheating; all your law and poets too.

Pan. Master high constable comes.

Enter TURFE.

Pup. I'll zay't afore hun.

Turfe. What's that makes you all so merry and loud, sirs, ha?
I could have heard you to my privy walk.

Clench. A contrevarsie 'twixt two learned men here:
Hannibal Puppy says that law and poetry
Are both flat cheating; all's but writing and reading,
He says, be't verse or prose.

Turfe. I think in conzience,
He do zay true: who is't do thwart 'un, ha?

Med. Why, my friend Scriben, an it please your worship.

Turfe. Who, D'oge, my D'ogenes? a great writer, marry!
He'll vace me down [sirs,] me myself sometimes,
That verse goes upon veet, as you and I do:
But I can gi''un the hearing; zit me down,
And laugh at 'un; and to myself conclude,
The greatest clerks are not the wisest men

Ever. Here they are both! what, sirs, disputing,
And holding arguments of verse and prose,
And no green thing afore the door, that shews,
Or speaks a wedding!

Scri. Those were verses now,
Your worship spake, and run upon vive veet.

- 14 -

Turfe. Feet, vrom my mouth, D'oge! leave your 'zurd upinions,
And get me in some boughs.

Scri. Let them have leaves first.
There's nothing green but bays and rosemary.

Pup. And they are too good for strewings, your maids say.

Turfe. You take up 'dority still to vouch against me.
All the twelve smocks in the house, zure, are your authors.
Get some fresh hay then, to lay under foot;
Some holly and ivy to make vine the posts:
Is't not zon Valentine's day, and mistress Awdrey,
Your young dame, to be married? *[Exit Puppy.]* I wonder Clay
Should be so tedious? he's to play son Valentine:
And the clown sluggard is not come fro' Kilborn yet!

Med. Do you call your son-in-law clown, an't please your
worship?

Turfe. Yes and vor worship too, my neighbour Medlay,
A Middlesex clown, and one of Finsbury.
They were the first colons of the kingdom here,
The primitory colons, my Diogenes says,
Where's D'ogenes, my writer, now? What were those
You told me, D'ogenes, were the first colons
Of the country, that the Romans brought in here? *Scri.* The
coloni, sir; *colonus* is an inhabitant,
A clown original: as you'd say, a farmer,
A tiller of the earth, e'er since the Romans
Planted their colony first; which was in Middlesex.

Turfe. Why so! I thank you heartily, good Diogenes,
You ha' zertified me. I had rather be
An ancient colon, (as they say,) a clown of Middlesex,
A good rich farmer, or high constable.
I'd play hun 'gain a knight, or a good 'squire,
Or gentleman of any other county
In the kingdom.

Pan. Outeept Kent, for there they landed
All gentlemen, and came in with the conqueror,
Mad Julius Cæsar, who built Dover-castle:
My ancestor To-Pan, beat the first kettle-drum
Avore 'hun, here vrom Dover on the march.
Which piece of monumental copper hangs
Up, scour'd, at Hammersmith yet; for there they came
Over the Thames, at a low water-mark;
Vore either London, ay, or Kingston-bridge,
I doubt, were kursin'd.

Re-enter PUPPY *with* JOHN CLAY.

Turfe. Zee, who is here: John Clay!
Zon Valentine, and bridegroom! have you zeen
Your Valentine-bride yet, sin' you came, John Clay?

Clay. No, wusse. Che lighted I but now in the yard,
Puppy has scarce unswaddled my legs yet.

Turfe. What, wisps on your wedding-day, zon! this is right
Originous Clay, and Clay o' Kilborn too!
I would ha' had boots on this day, zure, zon John.

Clay. I did it to save charges: we mun dance,
On this day, zure; and who can dance in boots?
No, I got on my best straw-colour'd stockings,
And swaddled them over to zave charges, I.

Turfe. And his new chamois doublet too witlnpoints!
I like that yet: and his long sausage-hose,
Like the commander of four smoking tile-kilns,
Which he is captain of, captain of Kilborn;
Clay with his hat turn'd up o' the leer side too,
As if he would leap my daughter yet ere night,
And spring a new Turfe to the old house! —

Enter JOYCE, JOAN, and the other Maids, with ribands, rosemary,
and bay for the bride-men.

Look! an the wenches ha' not found 'un out,
And do prazent 'un with a van of rosemary,
And bays, to vill a bow-pot, trim the head
Of my best vore-horse! we shall all ha' bride-laces.
Or points, I zee; my daughter will be valiant,
And prove a very Mary Ambry in the business.

Clench. They zaid your worship had 'sured her to 'squire Tub
Of Totten-Court here; all the hundred rings on't.

Turfe. A TALE OF A TUB, sir, a mere Tale of a Tub.
Lend it no ear, I pray you: the 'squire Tub
Is a fine man, but he is too fine a man,
And has a lady Tub too to his mother;
I'll deal with none of these fine silken Tubs:
John Clay and cloth-breech for my money and daughter.
Here eomes another old boy too vor his colours,

Enter ROSIN, and his two Boys.

Will stroak down my wive's udder of purses, empty
Ofall her milk-money this winter quarter:
Old father Rosin, the chief minstrel here,
Chief minstrel too of Highgate, she has hired him
And all his two boys for a day and a half;
And now they come for ribanding and rosemary:
Give them enough, girls, give them enough, and take it
Out in his tunes anon.

Clench. I'll have Tom Tiler,
For our John Clay's sake, and the tile-kilns, zure.

Med. And I the *Jolly Joiner* for mine own sake.

Pan. I'll have the *Jovial Tinker* for To-Pan's sake.

Turfe. We'll all be jovy this day vor son Valentine,
My sweet son John's sake. Scri. There's another reading now:
My master reads it Son and not Sin Valentine.

Pup. NorZim: and he's in the right; he is high constable,
And who should read above 'un, or avore hun?

Turfe. Son John shall bid us welcome all, this day;
We'll zerve under his colours: lead the troop, John,
And Puppy, see the bells ring. Press all noises
Of Finsbury, in our name: Diogenes Scriben
Shall draw a score of warrants vor the business.
Does any wight perzent hir majesty's person
This hundred, 'bove the high constable?

All. No, no.

Turfe. Use our authority then to the utmost on't. [*Exeunt.*

SCENE III

Maribone. – A Room in Justice PREAMBLE'S House.

Enter Canon HUGH and Justice PREAMBLE.

Hugh. So you are sure, sir, to prevent them all,
And throw a block in the bridegroom's way, John Clay,
That he will hardly leap o'er.

Pre. I conceive you,
Sir Hugh; as if your rhetoric would say,
Whereas the father of her is a Turfe,
A very superficies of the earth;
He aims no higher than to match in clay,
And there hath pitch'd his rest.

Hugh. Right, justice Bramble;
You have the winding wit, compassing all.

Pre. Subtle sir Hugh, you now are in the wrong,
And err with the whole neighbourhood, I must tell you,
For you mistake my name. Justice Preamble
I write myself; which, with the ignorant clowns here,
Because of my profession of the law,
And place of the peace, is taken to be Bramble:
But all my warrants, sir, do run Preamble,
Richard Preamble.

Hugh. Sir, I thank you for it,
That your good worship would not let me run
Longer in error, but would take me up thus.

Pre. You are my learned and canonic neighbour,
I would not have you stray; but the incorrigible
Nott-headed beast, the clowns, or constables,
Still let them graze, eat sallads, chew the cud:
All the town music will not move a log.

Hugh. The beetle and wedges will where you will have them.

Pre. True, true, sir Hugh. —

Enter METAPHOR.

Here comes Miles Metaphor,
My clerk; he is the man shall carry it, canon,
By my instructions.

Hugh. He will do it ad unguem,
Miles Metaphor! he is a pretty fellow.

Pre. I love not to keep shadows, or half-wits,
To foil a business. — Metaphor, you have seen
A king ride forth in state.

Met. Sir, that I have:
King Edward our late liege, and sovereign lord;
And have set down the pomp.

Pre. Therefore I ask'd you.
Have you observ'd the messengers of the chamber,
What habits they were in?

Met. Yes, minor coats,
Unto the guard, a dragon and a greyhound,
For the supporters of the arms.

Pre. Well mark'd!
You know not any of them?

Met. Here's one dwells
In Maribone.

Pre. Have you acquaintance with him,
To borrow his coat an hour?

Hugh. Or but his badge,
'Twill serve; a little thing he wears on his breast.

Pre. His coat, I say, is of more authority:
Borrow his coat for an hour. I do love
To do all things completely, canon Hugh;
Borrow his coat, Miles Metaphor, or nothing.

Met. The taberd of his office I will call it,
Or the coat-armour of his place; and so
Insinuate with him by that trope.

Pre. I know
Your powers of rhetoric, Metaphor. Fetch him off
In a fine figure for his coat, I say. *[Exit Metaphor.*

Hugh. I'll take my leave, sir, of your worship too,
Because I may expect the issue anon.

Pre. Stay, my diviner counsel, take your fee:
We that take fees, allow them to our counsel:
And our prime learned counsel, double fees.
There are a brace of angels to support you
In your foot-walk this frost, for fear of falling,
Or spraying of a point of matrimony,
When you come at it —

Hugh. In your worship's service:
That the exploit is done, and you possest
Of mistress Awdrey Turfe. —

Pre. I like your project. *[Exit.*

Hugh. And I, of this effect of two to one;
It worketh in my pocket, 'gainst the 'squire,
And his half bottom here, of half a piece,
Which was not worth the stepping o'er the stile for:
His mother has quite marr'd him, lady Tub,
She's such a vessel of faeces: all dried earth,
Terra damnata! not a drop of salt,
Or petre in her! all her nitre is gone. *[Exit.*

SCENE IV

      Totten-Court. — Before Lady TUB'S House.

      Enter Lady TUB and POL MARTIN.

Lady T. Is the nag ready, Martin? call the 'squire,
This frosty morning we will take the air,
About the fields; for I do mean to be
Somebody's Valentine, in my velvet gown,
This morning, though it be but a beggar-man.
Why stand you still, and do not call my son?

Pol. Madam, if he had couched with the lamb,
He had no doubt been stirring with the lark:
But he sat up at play, and watch'd the cock,
Till his first warning chid him off to rest.
Late watchers are no early wakers, madam:
But if your ladyship will have him call'd —

Lady T. Will have him call'd! wherefore did I, sir, bid him
Be call'd, you weazel, vermin of an huisher?
You will return your wit to your first stile
Of Martin Polecat, by these stinking tricks,
If you do use them; I shall no more call you
Pol Martin, by the title of a gentleman,
If you go on thus.

      Pol. I am gone. *[Exit.*

Lady T. Be quick then,
In your come off; and make amends, you stote!
Was ever such a fulmart for an huisher,
To a great worshipful lady, as myself!
Who, when I heard his name first, Martin Polecat,
A stinking name, and not to be pronounced
In any lady's presence without a reverence;
My very heart e'en yearn'd, seeing the fellow
Young, pretty, and handsome; being then, I say,
A basket-carrier, and a man condemn'd
To the salt-petre works; made it my suit
To master Peter Tub, that I might change it;
And call him as I do now, by Pol Martin,
To have it sound like a gentleman in an office,
And made him mine own foreman, daily waiter.
And he to serve me thus! ingratitude,
Beyond the coarseness yet of any clownage,
Shewn to a lady! —

Re-enter POL MARTIN.

What now, is he stirring?

Pol. Stirring betimes out of his bed, and ready.

Lady T. And comes he then?

Pol. No, madam, he is gone.

Lady T. Gone! whither? Ask the porter where is he gone.

Pol. I met the porter, and have ask'd him for him;
He says, he let him forth an hour ago.

Lady T. An hour ago! what business could he have
So early; where is his man, grave Basket-hilts,
His guide and governor?

Pol. Gone with his master.

Lady T. Is he gone too! O that same surly knave
Is his right-hand; and leads my son amiss.
He has carried him to some drinking match or other.
Pol Martin, — I will call you so again,
I am friends with you now — go, get your horse and ride
To all the towns about here, where his haunts are,
And cross the fields to meet, and bring me word;
He cannot be gone far, being a-foot.
Be curious to inquire him: and bid Wispe,
My woman, come, and wait on me. *[Exit Pol.]* The love
We mothers bear our sons we have brought with pain,
Makes us oft view them with too careful eyes,
And overlook them with a jealous fear,
Out-fitting mothers.

Enter DIDO WISPE.

Lady T. How now, Wispe! have you
A Valentine yet? I am taking the air to choose one.

Wispe. Fate send your ladyship a fit one then.

Lady T. What kind of one is that?

Wispe. A proper man
To please your ladyship.

Lady T. Out of that vanity
That takes the foolish eye! any poor creature,
Whose want may need my alms or courtesy,
I rather wish; so bishop Valentine
Left us example to do deeds of charity;
To feed the hungry, clothe the naked, visit
The weak and sick; to entertain the poor,
And give the dead a Christian funeral;
These were the works of piety he did practise,
And bade us imitate; not look for lovers,
Or handsome images to please our senses. —
I pray thee, Wispe, deal freely with me now,
We are alone, and may be merry a little:
Thou art none of the court glories, nor the wonders
For wit or beauty in the city; tell me,
What man would satisfy thy present fancy,
Had thy ambition leave to choose a Valentine,
Within the queen's dominion, so a subject?

Wispe. You have given me a large scope, madam, I confess,
And I will deal with your ladyship sincerely;
I'll utter my whole heart to you. I would have him
The bravest, richest, and the properest, man
A tailor could make up; or all the poets,
With the perfumers: I would have him such,
As not another woman but should spite me;
Three city ladies should run mad for him,
And country madams infinite.

Lady T. You would spare me,
And let me hold my wits?

Wispe. I should with you,
For the young 'squire, my master's sake, dispense
A little, but it should be very little.
Then all the court-wives I'd have jealous of me,
As all their husbands jealous too of them;
And not a lawyer's puss of any quality,
But lick her lips for a snatch in the term-time.

Lady T. Come,
Let's walk; we'll hear the rest as we go on:
You are this morning in a good vein, Dido;
Would I could be as merry! My son's absence
Troubles me not a little, though I seek
These ways to put it off; which will not help:
Care that is entered once into the breast,
Will have the whole possession ere it rest. [*Exeunt.*

ACT II

SCENE I

The Fields near PANCRAS.
Enter, in procession, with ribands, rosemary and bay, TURFE, CLAY MEDLAY, CLENCH, TO-PAN, SCRIBEN, and PUPPY with the bride-cake, as going to church.

Turfe. Zon Clay, cheer up, the better leg avore,
This is a veat is once done, and no more.

Clench. And then 'tis done vor ever, as they say.

Med. Right! vor a man has his hour, and a dog his day.

Turfe. True, neighbour Medlay, you are still In-and-in.

Med. I would be, master constable, if che could win.

Pan. I zay, John Clay keep still on his old gate:
Wedding and hanging both go at a rate.

Turfe. Well said, To-Pan: you have still the hap to hit
  The nail o' the head at a close: I think there never
  Marriage was managed with a more avisement,
Than was this marriage, though I say it that should not;
  Especially 'gain mine own flesh and blood,
  My wedded wife. Indeed my wife would ha' had
  All the young batchelors, and maids forsooth,
    Of the zix parishes hereabouts; but I
  Cried *none, sweet Sybil; none of that gear, I:*
    It would lick zalt, I told her, by her leave.
No, three or vour our wise, choice, honest neighbours,
  Ubstantial persons, men that have born office,
   And mine own family would be enough
  To eat our dinner. What! dear meat's a thief;
  I know it by the butchers and the market-volk.
   Hum drum, I cry. No half ox in a pye:
  A man that's bid to a bride-ale, if he have cake
  And drink enough, he need not vear his stake.
Clench. 'Tis right; he has spoke as true as a gun, believe it.

Enter Dame TURFE and AWDREY, followed by JOAN, JOYCE, MADGE PARNEL, GRISEL, and KATE, dressed for the wedding.

Turfe. Come, Sybil, come; did not I tell you o' this,
  This pride and muster of women would mar all?
    Six women to one daughter, and a mother!
   The queen (God save her) ha' no more herself.

Dame T. Why, if you keep so many, master Turfe,
  Why should not all present our service to her?

Turfe. Your service! good! I think you'll write to her shortly,
    Your very loving and obedient mother.
  Come, send your maids off, I will have them sent
    Home again, wife; I love no trains of Kent,
      Or Christendom, as they say.

Joyce. We will not back,
And leave our dame.

Madge. Why should her worship lack
Her tail of maids, more than you do of men?

Turfe. What, mu tilling, Madge?

Joan. Zend back your clowns agen,
And we will vollow.

All. Else we'll guard our dame.

Turfe. I ha' zet the nest of wasps all on a flame.

Dame T. Come, you are such another, master Turfe,
A clod you should be call'd, of a high constable:
To let no music go afore your child
To church, to chear her heart up this cold morning!

Turfe. You are for father Rosin and his consort
Of Fiddling boys, the great Feates and the less;
Because you have entertain'd them all from Highgate.
To shew your pomp, you'd have your daughters and maids
Dance o'er the fields like faies to church, this frost.
I'll have no rondels, I, in the queen's paths;
Let 'em scrape the gut at home, where they have fill'd it,
At afternoon.

Dame T. I'll have them play at dinner.

Clench. She is in the right, sir; vor your wedding-dinner
Is starv'd without the music.

Med. If the pies
Come not in piping hot, you have lost that proverb.

Turfe. I yield to truth: wife, are you sussified?

Pan. A right good man! when he knows right, he loves it.

Seri. And he will know't and shew't too by his place
Of being high constable, if no where else.

Enter HILTS, with a false beard, booted and spurred.

Hilts. Well overtaken, gentlemen! I pray you
Which is the queen's high constable among you?

Pup. The tallest man; who should be else, do you think?

Hilts. It is no matter what I think, young clown;
Your answer savours of the cart.

Pup. How! *cart*
And *clown!* do you know whose team you speak to?

Hilts. No, nor I care not: Whose jade may you be?

Pup. Jade! *cart!* and *clown!* O for a lash of whip-cord,
Three-knotted cord!

Hilts. Do you mutter! sir, snorle this way,
That I may hear, and answer what you say,
With my school-dagger 'bout your costard, sir.
Look to't, young growse: I'll lay it on, and sure;
Take't off who wuil. *[Draws his sword.*

Clench. Nay, 'pray you, gentleman —

Hilts. Go to, I will not bate him an ace on't.
What rowly-powly, maple face! all fellows!

Pup. Do you hear, friend? I would wish you, for your good,
Tie up your brended bitch there, your dun, rusty,
Pannier-hilt poniard; and not vex the youth
With shewing the teeth of it. We now are going
To church in way of matrimony, some on us;
They ha' rung all in a' ready. If it had not,
All the horn-beasts are grazing in this close
Should not have pull'd me hence, till this ash-plant
Had rung noon on your pate, master Broombeard.

Hilts. That I would fain zee, quoth the blind George
Of Holloway: come, sir.

Awd. O their naked weapons!

Pan. For the passion of man, hold gentleman and Puppy.

Clay. Murder, O murder!

Awd. O my father and mother!

Dame T. Husband, what do you mean? son Clay, for God's
sake —

Turfe. I charge you in the queen's name, keep the peace.

Hilts. Tell me o' no queen or keysar; I must have
A leg or a hanch of him ere I go.

Med. But, zir,
You must obey the queen's high officers.

Hilts. Why must I, goodman Must?

Med. You must an' you wull.

Turfe. Gentlemen, I am here for fault, high constable —

Hilts. Are you zo! what then?

Turfe. I pray you, sir, put up
Your weapons; do, at my request: for him,
On my authority, he shall lie by the heels,
Verbatim continente, an I live.

Dame T. Out on him for a knave, what a dead fright
He has put me into! come, Awdrey, do not shake.

Awd. But is not Puppy hurt, nor the t'other man?

Clay. No bun? but had not I cried murder, I wuss —

Pup. Sweet goodman Clench, I pray you revise my master,
I may not zit in the stocks till the wedding be past,
Dame, mistress Awdrey: I shall break the bride-cake else.

Clench. Zomething must be to save authority, Puppy.

Dame T. Husband —

Clench. And gossip —

Awd. Father —

Turfe. Treat me not,
It is in vain. If he lie not by the heels,
I'll lie there for 'un; I will teach the hind
To carry a tongue in his head to his superiors.

Hilts. This's a wise constable! where keeps he school?

Clench. In Kentish-town; a very servere man.

Hilts. But, as servere as he is, let me, sir, tell him
He shall not lay his man by the heels for this.
This was my quarrel; and by his office' leave,
If it carry 'un for this, it shall carry double;
Vor he shall carry me too.

Turfe. Breath of man!
He is my chattel, mine own hired goods:
An if you do abet 'un in this matter,
I'll clap you both by the heels, ankle to ankle.

Hilts. You'll clap a dog of wax as soon, old Blurt.
Come, spare not me, sir, I am no man's wife;
I care not, I, sir, not three skips of a louse for you,
An you were ten tall constables, not I.

Turfe. Nay, pray you, sir, be not angry, but content;
My man shall make you what amends you'll ask 'un.

Hilts. Let 'un mend his manners then, and know his betters;
It's all I ask 'un; and 'twill be his own,
And's master's too another day; che vore 'un.

Med. As right as a club still! Zure this angry man
Speaks very near the mark when he is pleased.

Pup. I thank you, sir, an' I meet you at Kentish-town,
   I ha' the courtesy o' the hundred for you.

Hilts. Gramercy, good high constable's hind! But hear you?
   Mass constable, I have other manner of matter
   To bring you about than this. And so it is,
   I do belong to one of the queen's captains,
   A gentleman o' the field, one captain Thums,
   I know not whether you know 'un or no: it may be
   You do, and it may be you do not again.

Turfe. No, I assure you on my constableship,
   I do not know 'un.

   Hilts. Nor I neither, i'faith. —
   It skills not much; my captain and myself
   Having occasion to come riding by here
   This morning, at the corner of St. John's-wood,
   Some mile [west] o' this town, were set upon
   By a sort of country-fellows, that not only
   Beat us, but robb'd us most sufficiently,
   And bound us to our behaviour hand and foot;
   And so they left us. Now, don constable,
   I am to charge you in her majesty's name,
   As you will answer it at your apperil,
That forthwith you raise hue and cry in the hundred,
   For all such persons as you can despect,
By the length and breadth of your office: for I tell you,
   The loss is of some value; therefore look to't.

Turfe. As fortune mend me now, or any office
Of a thousand pound, if I know what to zay.
Would I were dead, or vaire hang'd up at Tyburn,
If I do know what course to take, or how
To turn myself just at this time too, now
My daughter is to be married! I'll but go
To Pancridge-church hard by, and return instantly,
And all my neighbourhood shall go about it.

Hilts. Tut, Pancridge me no Pancridge! if you let it
Slip, you will answer it, an your cap be of wool;
Therefore take heed, you'll feel the smart else, constable.
[*Going.*

Turfe. Nay, good sir, stay. — Neighbours, what think you of this?

Dame T. Faith, man —

Turfe. Odds precious, woman, hold your tongue,
And mind your pigs on the spit at home; you must
Have [an] oar in every thing. — Pray you, sir, what kind
Of fellows were they?

Hilts. Thieves-kind, I have told you.

Turfe. I mean, what kind of men?

Hilts. Men of our make.

Turfe. Nay, but with patience, sir: We that are officers
Must 'quire the special marks, and all the tokens
Of the despected parties; or perhaps else
Be ne'er the near of our purpose in 'prehending them.
Can you tell what 'parrel any of them wore?

Hilts. Troth, no; there were so many o"em all like
So one another; now I remember me,
There was one busy fellow was their leader,
A blunt squat swad, but lower than yourself;
He had on a leather-doublet with long points,
And a pair of pinn'd-up breeches, like pudding-bags
With yellow stockings, and his hat turn'd up
With a silver clasp on his leer side.

Dame T. By these
Marks it should be John Clay, now bless the man!

Turfe. Peace, and be nought! I think the woman be phrensic.

Hilts. John Clay! what's he, good mistress?

Awd. He that shall be
My husband.

Hilts. How! your husband, pretty one?

Awd. Yes, I shall anon be married; that is he.

Turfe. Passion o' me, undone!

Pup. Bless master's son!

Hilts. O, you are well 'prehended: know you me, sir?

Clay. No's my record; I never zaw you avore.

Hilts. You did not! where were your eyes then, out at washing?

Turfe. What should a man zay, who should he trust
    In these days? Hark you, John Clay, if you have
    Done any such thing, tell troth and shame the devil.

Clench. Yaith, do; my gossip Turfe zays well to you, John.

Med. Speak, man; but do not convess, nor be avraid.

Pan. A man is a man, and a beast's a beast, look to't.

Dame T. In the name of men or beasts, what do you do?
    Hare the poor fellow out on his five wits,
    And seven senses! do not weep, John Clay.
    I swear the poor wretch is as guilty from it
    As the child was, was born this very morning.

Clay. No, as I am a kyrsin soul, would I were hang'd
    If ever I alas, I would I were out
    Of my life; so I would I were, and in again —

Pup. Nay, mistress Awdrey will say nay to that;
    No, in-and-out: an you were out of your life,
    How should she do for a husband? who should fall
    Aboard of her then? — Ball? he's a puppy!
    No, Hannibal has no breeding! well, I say little;
But hitherto all goes well, pray it prove no better. [*Aside.*

Awd. Come, father; I would we were married! I am a-cold.

Hilts. Well, master constable, this your fine groom here,
Bridegroom, or what groom else soe'er he be,
I charge him with the felony, and charge you
To carry him back forthwith to Paddington
Unto my captain, who stays my return there:
I am to go to the next justice of peace,
To get a warrant to raise hue and cry,
And bring him and his fellows all afore 'un.
Fare you well, sir, and look to 'un, I charge you
As you will answer it. Take heed; the business
If you defer, may prejudicial you
More than you think for; zay I told you so. *[Exit.*

Turfe. Here's a bride-ale indeed! ah, zon John, zon Clay!
I little thought you would have proved a piece
Of such false metal.

Clay. Father, will you believe me?
Would I might never stir in my new shoes,
If ever I would do so voul a fact.

Turfe. Well, neighbours, I do charge you to assist me
With 'un to Paddington. Be he a true man, so!
The better for 'un. I will do mine office,
An he were my own begotten a thousand times.

Dame T. Why, do you hear, man? husband, master Turfe!
What shall my daughter do? Puppy, stay here.
[Exeunt all but Awdrey and Puppy.

Awd. Mother, I'll go with you and with my father.

Pup. Nay, stay, sweet mistress Awdrey: here are none
But one friend, as they zay, desires to speak
A word or two, cold with you: how do you veel
Yourself this frosty morning?

Awd. What have you
To do to ask, I pray you? I am a-cold.

Pup. It seems you are hot, good mistress Awdrey.

Awd. You lie; I am as cold as ice is, feel else.

Pup. Nay, you have cool'd my courage; I am past it,
I ha' done feeling with you.

Awd. Done with me!
I do defy you, so I do, to say
You ha' done with me: you are a saucy Puppy.

Pup. O you mistake! I meant not as you mean.

Awd. Meant you not knavery, Puppy?

Pup. No, not I.
Clay meant you all the knavery, it seems,
Who rather than he would be married to you,
Chose to be wedded to the gallows first.

Awd. I thought he was a dissembler; he would prove
A slippery merchant in the frost. He might
Have married one first, and have been hang'd after,
If he had had a mind to't. But you men —
Fie on you!

Pup. Mistress Awdrey, can you vind
In your heart to fancy Puppy? me poor Ball?

Awd. You are disposed to jeer one, master Hannibal. —

Re-enter HILTS.

Pity o' me, the angry man with the beard!

Hilts. Put on thy hat, I look for no despect.
Where is thy master?

Pup. Marry, he is gone
With the picture of despair to Paddington.

Hilts. Prithee run after 'un, and tell 'un he shall
Find out my captain lodged at the Red-Lion,
In Paddington; that's the inn. Let 'un ask
Vor captain Thums; and take that for thy pains:
He may seek long enough else. Hie thee again.

Pup. Yes, sir; you'll look to mistress bride the while?

Hilts. That I will: prithee haste. *[Exit Puppy.*

Awd. What, Puppy! Puppy!

Hilts. Sweet mistress bride, he'll come again presently. —
Here was no subtle device to get a wench!
This Canon has a brave pate of his own,
A shaven pate, and a right monger y' vaith;
This was his plot. I follow captain Thums!
We robb'd in St. John's-wood! In my t'other hose! —
I laugh to think what a fine fool's finger they have
O' this wise constable, in pricking out
This captain Thums to his neighbours: you shall see
The tile-man too set fire on his own kiln,
And leap into it to save himself from hanging.
You talk of a bride-ale, here was a bride-ale broke
In the nick! Well, I must yet dispatch this bride
To mine own master, the young 'squire, and then
My task is done. — [*Aside.*] — Gentlewoman, I have in sort
Done you some wrong, but now I'll do you what right
I can: it's true, you are a proper woman;
But to be oast away on such a clown-pipe
As Clay! methinks your friends are not so wise
As nature might have made 'em; well, go to:
There's better fortune coming towards you,
An you do not deject it. Take a vool's
Counsel, and do not stand in your own light;
It may prove better than you think for, look you.

Awd. Alas, sir, what is't you would have me do?
I'd fain do all for the best, if I knew how.

Hilts. Forsake not a good turn when it is offer'd you,
Fair mistress Awdrey — that's your name, I take it.

Awd. No mistress, sir, my name is Awdrey.

Hilts. Well; so it is, there is a bold young 'squire,
The blood of Totten, Tub, and Tripoly —
Awd. 'Squire Tub, you mean: I know him, he knows me too.

Hilts. He is in love with you; and more, he's mad for you.

Awd. Ay, so he told me in his wits, I think.
But he's too fine for me; and has a lady
Tub to his mother.

Enter Tub.

Here he comes himself!

Tub. O you are a trusty governor!

Hilts. VVhat ails you?
You do not know when you are well, I think.
You'd ha' the calf with the white face, sir, would you?
I have her for you here; what would you more?

Tub. Quietness, Hilts, and hear no more of it.

Hilts. No more of it, quoth you! I do not care
If some on us had not heard so much of it.
I tell you true; a man must carry and vetch
Like fiungy's dog for you.

Tub. What's he?

Hilts. A spaniel —
And scarce be spit in the mouth for't. A good dog
 Deserves, sir, a good bone, of a free master;
 But, an your turns be serv'd, the devil a bit
 You care for a man after, e'er a laird of you.
Like will to like, y-faith, quoth the scabb'd 'squire
 To the mangy knight, when both met in a dish
 Of butter'd vish. One bad, there's ne'er a good;
And not a barrel the better herring among you.

Tub. Nay, Hilts, I pray thee grow not frampull now.
 Turn not the bad cow after thy good soap.
 Our plot hath hitherto ta'en good effect,
 And should it now be troubled or stopp'd up,
 'Twould prove the utter ruin of my hopes.
 I pray thee haste to Pancridge, to the Canon,
 And give him notice of our good success.
 Will him that all things be in readiness:
 Fair Awdrey and myself will cross the fields
The nearest path. Good Hilts, make thou some haste,
And meet us on the way. — Come, gentle Awdrey.

Hilts. Yaith, would I had a few more geances on't!
 An you say the word, send me to Jericho.
Outcept a man were a post-horse, I have not known
 The like on it; yet, an he had [had] kind words,
 'Twould never irke 'un: but a man may break
 His heart out in these days, and get a flap
With a fox-tail, when he has done — and there is all!

Tub. Nay, say not so, Hilts: hold thee, there are crowns
 My love bestows on thee for thy reward;
 If gold will please thee, all my land shall drop
 In bounty thus, to recompense thy merit.

Hilts. Tut, keep your land, and your gold too, sir, I
    Seek neither — neither of 'un. Learn to get
More; you will know to spend that zuin you have
    Early enough; you are assured of me:
I love you too too well to live o' the spoil —
For your own sake, would there were no worse than I!
All is not gold that glisters. I'll to Pancridge. *[Exit crying.*

Tub. See how his love does melt him into tears!
    An honest faithful servant is a jewel. —
Now the advent'rous 'squire hath time and leisure
    To ask his Awdrey how she does, and hear
A grateful answer from her. She not speaks. —
Hath the proud tyrant Frost usurp'd the seat
    Of former beauty, in my love's fair cheek;
Staining the roseate tincture of her blood
    With the dull dye of blue congealing cold?
No, sure the weather dares not so presume
    To hurt an object of her brightness. Yet,
The more I view her, she but looks so, so.
Ha! give me leave to search this mystery —
O now I have it: Bride, I know your grief;
The last night's cold hath bred in you such horror
    Of the assigned bridegroom's constitution,
The Kilborn clay-pit; that frost-bitten marl,
That lump in courage, melting cake of ice:
That the conceit thereof hath almost kill'd thee:
But I must do thee good, wench, and refresh thee.

Awd. You are a merry man, 'squire Tub of Totten!
I have heard much o' your words, but not o' your deeds.

Tub. Thou sayst true, sweet; I have been too slack in deeds.

Awd. Yet I was never so strait-laced to you, 'squire.

Tub. Why, did you ever love me, gentle Awdrey?

Awd. Love you! I cannot tell: I must hate no body,
My father says.

Tub. Yes, Clay and Kilborn, Awdrey,
You must hate them.

Awd. It shall be for your sake then.

Tub. And for my sake shall yield you that gratuity.
[*Offers to kiss her.*

Awd. Soft and fair, 'squire, there go two words to a bargain.
[*Puts him back.*

Tub. What are those, Awdrey?

Awd. Nay, I cannot tell.
My mother said, zure, if you married me,
You'd make me a lady the first week; and put me
In — I know not what, the very day.

Tub. What was it?
Speak, gentle Awdrey, thou shalt have it yet.

Awd. A velvet dressing for my head, it is,
They say, will make one brave; I will not know
Bess Moale, nor Margery Turn-up: I will look
Another way upon them, and be proud.

Tub. Troth, I could wish my wench a better wit;
But what she wanteth there, her face supplies.
There is a pointed lustre in her eye
Hath shot quite through me, and hath hit my heart:
And thence it is I first received the wound,
That rankles now, which only she can cure.
Fain would I work myself from this conceit;
But, being flesh, I cannot. I must love her,
The naked truth is; and I will go on,
Were it for nothing but to cross my rivals. *[Aside.*
Come, Awdrey, I am now resolv'd to have thee.

Enter Justice PREAMBLE, *and* METAPHOR *disguised as a pursuivant.*

Pre. Nay, do it quickly, Miles; why shak'st thou, man?
Speak but his name, I'll second thee myself.

Met. What is his name?
Pre. 'Squire Tripoly, or Tub;
Any thing —
Met. 'Squire Tub, I do arrest you
In the queen's majesty's name, and all the council's.

Tub. Arrest me, varlet!

Pre. Keep the peace, I charge you.

Tub. Are you there, justice Bramble! where's your warrant?

Pre. The warrant is directed here to me,
From the whole table; wherefore I would pray you,
Be patient, 'squire, and make good the peace.

Tub. Well, at your pleasure, justice. I am wrong'd:
Sirrah, what are you have arrested me?

Pre. He is a pursuivant at arms, 'squire Tub.

Met. I am a pursuivant; see by my coat else.

Tub. Well, pursuivant, go with me: I'll give you bail.

Pre. Sir, he may take no bail: it is a warrant
In special from the council, and commands
Your personal appearance. Sir, your weapon
I must require; and then deliver you
A prisoner to this officer, 'squire Tub.
I pray you to conceive of me no other,
Than as your friend and neighbour: let my person
Be sever'd from my office in the fact,
And I am clear. Here, pursuivant, receive him
Into your hands, and use him like a gentleman.

Tub. I thank you, sir: but whither must I go now?

Pre. Nay, that must not be told you till you come
Unto the place assign'd by his instructions:
I'll be the maiden's convoy to her father,
For this time, 'squire.

Tub. I thank you, master Bramble.
I doubt or fear you will make her the balance
To weigh your justice in. Pray ye do me right,
And lead not her, at least, out of the way:
Justice is blind, and having a blind guide,
She may be apt to slip aside.

Pre. I'll see to her. [Exit Pre with Awd.

Tub. I see my wooing will not thrive. Arrested,
As I had set my rest up for a wife!
And being so fair for it as I was! — Well, fortune,
Thou art a blind bawd and a beggar too,
To cross me thus; and let my only rival
To get her from me! that's the spight of spights.
But most I muse at, is, that I, being none
O' the court, am sent for thither by the council:
My heart is not so light as it was in the morning.

Re-enter HILTS.

Hilts. You mean to make a hoiden or a hare
Of me, to hunt counter thus, and make these doubles:
And you mean no such thing as you send about.
Where is your sweet heart now, I marie?

Tub. Oh Hilts!

Hilts. I know you of old! ne'er halt afore a cripple.
Will you have a caudle? where's your grief, sir? speak.

Met. Do you hear, friend, do you serve this gentleman?

Hilts. How then, sir? what if I do? peradventure yea,
Peradventure nay; what's that to you, sir? say.

Met. Nay, pray you, sir, I meant no harm in truth;
But this good gentleman is arrested.

Hilts. How!
Say me that again.

Tub. Nay, Basket, never storm;
I am arrested here, upon command
From the queen's council; and I must obey.

Met. You say, sir, very true, you must obey.
An honest gentleman, in faith.

Hilts. He must!

Tub. But that which most tormenteth me is this,
That justice Bramble hath got hence my Awdrey.

Hilts. How! how! stand by a little, sirrah, you
With the badge on your breast. *[Draws his sword.]* Let's know,
sir, what you are.

Met. I am, sir, — pray you do not look so terribly —
A pursuivant.

Hilts. A pursuivant! your name, sir?

Met. My name, sir —

Hilts. Whatis't? speak.

Met. Miles Metaphor;
And justice Preamble's clerk.

Tub. What says he?

Hilts. Pray you,
Let us alone. You are a pursuivant?

Met. No, faith, sir, would I might never stir from you,
I is made a pursuivant against my will.

Hilts. Ha! and who made you one? tell true, or my will
    Shall make you nothing instantly.

        Met. [*kneels.*] Put up
Your frightful blade, and your dead-doing look,
    And I shall tell you all.

        Hilts. Speak then the truth,
And the whole truth, and nothing but the truth.

Met. My master, justice Bramble, hearing your master,
    The 'squire Tub, was coming on this way,
With mistress Awdrey, the high constable's daughter,
    Made me a pursuivant, and gave me warrant
    To arrest him; so that he might get the lady,
With whom he is gone to Pancridge, to the vicar,
    Not to her father's. This was the device,
    Which I beseech you do not tell my master.

Tub. O wonderful! well, Basket, let him rise;
    And for my free escape forge some excuse.
    I'll post to Paddington to acquaint old Turfe
With the whole business, and so stop the marriage. [*Exit.*

Hilts. Well, bless thee: I do wish thee grace to keep
    Thy master's secrets better, or be hang'd.

Met. [*rises.*] I thank you for your gentle admonition.
    Pray you, let me call you god-father hereafter:
    And as your godson Metaphor, I promise
    To keep my master's privities seal'd up
In the vallies of my trust, lock'd close for ever,
    Or let me be truss'd up at Tyburn shortly.

Hilts. Thine own wish save or choke thee! come away. *[Exeunt.*

ACT III

SCENE I

KENTISH-TOWN. *tauter* TURFE, CLENCH, MEDLAY, TO-
PAN, SCRIBEN, *and* CLAY.

Turfe. Passion of me, was ever a man thus cross'd!
All things run arsie versie, up-side down.
High constable! now by our lady of Walsingham,
I had rather be mark'd out Tom Scavinger,
And with a shovel make clean the highways,
Than have this office of a constable,
And a high constable! the higher charge,
It brings more trouble, more vexation with it.
Neighbours, good neighbours, 'vize me what to do;
How we shall bear us in this hue and cry.
We cannot find the captain, no such man
Lodged at the Lion, nor came thither hurt,
The morning we have spent in privy search;
And by that means the bride-ale is deferr'd:
The bride, she's left alone in Puppy's charge;
The bridegroom goes under a pair of sureties,
And held of all as a respected person.
How should we bustle forward? give some counsel
How to bestir our stumps in these cross ways.

Clench. Faith, gossip Turfe, you have, you say, remission
To comprehend all such as are despected:
Now would I make another privy search
Thorough this town, and then you have search'd two towns.

Med. Masters, take heed, let us not vind too many:
One is enough to stay the hangman's stomach.
There is John Clay, who is yvound already,
A proper man, a tile-man by his trade,
A man, as one would zay, moulded in clay;
As spruce as any neighbour's child among you:
And he (you zee) is taken on conspition,
And two or three, they zay, what call you 'em?
Zuch as the justices of *coram nobis*
Grant — I forget their names, you have many on 'em,
Master high constable, they come to you. —
I have it at my tongue's ends — coney-boroughs,
To bring him strait avore the zessions-house.

Turfe. O you mean warrens, neighbour, do you not?

Med. Ay, ay, thik same! you know 'em well enough.

Turfe. Too well, too well: would I had never known them!
We good vreeholders cannot live in quiet,
But every hour new purcepts, hues and cries,
Put us to requisitions night and day —
What shud a man say? shud we leave the zearch,
I am in danger to reburse as much
As he was robb'd on; ay, and pay his hurts.
If I should vollow it, all the good cheer
That was provided for the wedding-dinner
Is spoil'd and lost. O, there are two vat pigs
A zindging by the vire: now by St. Tony,
Too good to eat, but on a wedding-day;
And then a goose will bid you all, come cut me.
Zon Clay, zon Clay, for I must call thee so,
Be of good comfort: take my muckinder,
And dry thine eyes. If thou be'st true and honest,
And if thou find'st thy conscience clear vrom it,
Pluck up a good heart, we'll do well enough:
If not, confess a-truth's name. But in faith,
I durst be sworn upon all holy books,
John Clay would ne'er commit a robbery
On his own head.

Clay. No, truth is my rightful judge;
I have kept my hands herehence from evil-speaking,
Lying, and slandering; and my tongue from stealing.
He do not live this day can say, John Clay,
I have zeen thee, but in the way of honesty.

Pan. Faith, neighbour Medlay, I durst be his burrough,
He would not look a true man in the vace.

Clay. I take the town to concord, where I dwell,
All Kilborn be my witness, if I were not
Begot in bashfulness, brought up in shamefacedness.
Let 'un bring a dog but to my vace that can
Zay I have beat 'un, and without a vault;
Or but a cat will swear upon a book,
I have as much as zet a vire her tail,
And I'll give him or her a crown for 'mends.
But to give out and zay I have robb'd a captain!
Receive me at the latter day, if I
E'er thought of any such matter, or could mind it.

Med. No, John, you are come of too good personage:
I think my gossip Clench and master Turfe
Both think you would ratempt no such voul matter.

Turfe. But how unhappily it comes to pass
Just on the wedding-day! I cry me mercy,
I had almost forgot the hue and cry:
Good neighbour Pan, you are the thirdborough,
And D'ogenes Scriben, you my learned writer,
Make out a new purcept — Lord for thy goodness,
I had forgot my daughter all this while!
The idle knave hath brought no news from her.
Here comes the sneaking puppy. —

Enter Puppy and Dame Turfe, on different sides.

What's the news?
My heart! my heart! I fear all is not well,
Something's mishapp'd; that he is come without her.

Pup. O, where's my master, my master, my master?

Dame T. Thy master! what would'st have with thy master, man?
There is thy master.

Turfe. What's the matter. Puppy?

Pup. O master, oh dame! oh dame! oh master!

Dame T. What say'st thou to thy master or thy dame?

Pup. Oh John Clay, John Clay, John Clay!

Turfe. What of John Clay?

Med. Luck grant he bring not news he shall be hang'd!

Clench. The world forfend! I hope it is not so well.

Clay. O Lord! oh me! what shall I do? poor John!

Pup. Oh John Clay, John Clay, John Clay!

Clay. Alas,
That ever I was born! I will not stay by't,
For all the tiles in Kilborn. [*Runs off.*

Dame T. What of Clay?
Speak, Puppy; what of him?

Pup. He hath lost, he hath lost —

Turfe. For luck sake speak, Puppy, what hath he lost!

Pup. Oh Awdrey, Awdrey, Awdrey!

Dame T. What of my daughter Awdrey?

Pup. I tell you, Awdrey — do you understand me?
Awdrey, sweet master, Awdrey, my dear dame —

Turfe. Where is she? what's become of her, I pray thee?

Pup. Oh, the serving-man, the serving-man, the serving-man!

Turfe. What talk'st thou of the serving-man! where's Awdrey?

Pup. Gone with the serving-man, gone with the serving-man.

Dame T. Good Puppy, whither is she gone with him?

Pup. I cannot tell: he bade me bring you word
The captain lay at the Lion, and before
I came again, Awdrey was gone with the serving-man;
I tell you, Awdrey's run away with the serving-man.
Turfe. 'Od'socks, my woman, what shall we do now?

Dame T. Now, so you help not, man, I know not, I.

Turfe. This was your pomp of maids! I told you on't.
Six maids to vollow you, and not leave one
To wait upon your daughter! I zaid pride
Would be paid one day her old vi'pence, wife.

Med. What of John Clay, Ball Puppy?

Pup. He hath lost —

Med. His life for velony?

Pup. No, his wife by villainy.

Turfe. Now villains both! oh that same hue and cry!
Oh neighbours! oh that cursed serving-man!
O maids! O wife! but John Clay, where is he? —
How! fled for fear, zay ye? will he slip us now?
We that are sureties must require 'un out.
How shall we do to find the serving-man?
Cock's bodikins, we must not lose John Clay;
Awdrey, my daughter Awdrey too! let us zend
To all the towns and zeek her; — but, alas,
The hue and cry, that must be look'd unto.

Enter TUB.

Tub. What, in a passion, Turfe?

Turfe. Ay, good 'squire Tub.
Were never honest varmers thus perplext.

Tub. Turfe, I am privy to thy deep unrest:
The ground of which springs from an idle plot,
Cast by a suitor to your daughter Awdrey —
And thus much, Turfe, let me advertise you;
Your daughter Awdrey met I on the way,
With justice Bramble in her company;
Who means to marry her at Pancras-church.
And there is canon Hugh to meet them ready:
Which to prevent, you must not trust delay;
But winged speed must cross their sly intent:
Then hie thee, Turfe, haste to forbid the banes.

Turfe. Hath justice Bramble got my daughter Awdrey?
A little while shall he enjoy her, zure.
But O, the hue and cry! that hinders me;
I must pursue that, or neglect my journey:
I'll e'en leave all, and with the patient ass,
The over-laden ass, throw off my burden,
And cast mine office: pluck in my large ears
Betimes, lest some disjudge 'em to be horns:
I'll leave to beat it on the broken hoof,
And ease my pasterns; I'll no more high constables.

Tub. I cannot choose but smile to see thee troubled
With such a bald, half-hatched circumstance.
The captain was not robb'd, as is reported;
That trick the justice craftily devised,
To break the marriage with the tileman Clay.
The hue and cry was merely counterfeit:
The rather may you judge it to be such,
Because the bridegroom was described to be
One of the thieves first in the felony;
Which, how far 'tis from him, yourselves may guess.
'Twas justice Bramble's fetch to get the wench.

Turfe. And is this true, 'squire Tub?

Tub. Believe me, Turfe,
As I am a 'squire; or less, a gentleman.

Turfe. I take my office back, and my authority,
Upon your worship's words: — Neighbours, I am
High constable again. Where's my zon Clay?
He shall be zon yet; wife, your meat by leisure:
Draw back the spits.

Dame T. That's done already, man.

Turfe. I'll break this marriage off; and afterward,
She shall be given to her first betroth'd.
Look to the meat, wife, look well to the roast.
[*Exit, followed by his neighbours.*

Tub. I'll follow him aloof to see the event. [*Exit.*

Pup. Dame, mistress, though I do not turn the spit,
I hope yet the pig's head.

Dame T. Come up, Jack sauce;
It shall be serv'd into you.

Pup. No, no service,
But a reward for service.

Dame T. I still took you
For an unmannerly Puppy: will you come,
And vetch more wood to the vire, master Ball? *[Exit.*

Pup. I, wood to the vire! I shall piss it out first:
You think to make me e'en your ox or ass,
Or any thing: though I cannot right myself
On you, I'll sure revenge me on your meat. *[Exit.*

SCENE II

The same. — Before TUBFE'S House.

Enter Lady TUB, POL MARTIN, and WISPE.

Pol. Madam, to Kentish-town we are got at length;
But by the way we cannot meet the 'squire,
Nor by inquiry can we hear of him.
Here is Turfe's house, the father of the maid.

Lady T. Pol Martin, see! the streets are strew'd with herbs;
And here hath been a wedding, Wispe, it seems.
Pray heaven this bride-ale be not for my son!
Good Martin, knock, knock quickly; ask for Turfe.
My thoughts misgive me, I am in such a doubt —

Pol. [*knocking.*] Who keeps the house here?

Pup. [*within.*] Why the door and walls
Do keep the house.

Pol. I ask then, who's within?

Pup. [*within.*] Not you that are without.

Pol. Look forth, and speak
Into the street here. Come before my lady.

Pup. [*within.*] Before my lady! Lord have mercy upon me:
If I do come before her, she will see
The handsomest man in all the town, pardee!

Enter PUPPY from the house.

Now stand I vore her, what zaith velvet she?

Lady T. Sirrah, whose man are you?

Pup. Madam, my master's.

Lady T. And who's thy master?

Pup. What you tread on, madam.

Lady T. I tread on an old Turfe.

Pup. That Turfe's my master.

Lady T. A merry fellow! what's thy name?

Pup. Ball Puppy
They call me at home: abroad Hannibal Puppy.

Lady T. Come hither, I must kiss thee, valentine Puppy.
Wispe, have you got a valentine?

Wispe. None, madam:
He's the first stranger that I saw.

Lady T. To me
He is so, and as such, let's share him equally.
[*They struggle to kiss him.*

Pup. Help, help, good dame! A rescue, and in time.
Instead of bills, with colstaves come; instead of spears, with spits;
Your slices serve for slicing swords, to save me and my wits:
A lady and her woman here, their huisher eke by side,
(But he stands mute,) have plotted how your Puppy to divide.

Enter Dame TURFE, JOAN, JOYCE, MADGE, etc.

Dame T. How now, what noise is this with you, Ball Puppy?

Pup. Oh dame, and fellows of the kitchen! arm,
Arm, for my safety; if you love your Ball:
Here is a strange thing call'd a lady, a mad-dame,
And a device of hers, yclept her woman,
Have plotted on me in the king's highway,
To steal me from myself, and cut me in halfs,
To make one valentine to serve them both;
This for my right-side, that my left-hand love.

Dame T. So saucy, Puppy! to use no more reverence
Unto my lady and her velvet gown?

Lady T. Turfe's wife, rebuke him not; your man doth please me
With his conceit: hold, there are ten old nobles,
To make thee merrier yet, half-valentine.

Pup. I thank you, right-side; could my left as much,
'Twould make me a man of mark, young Hannibal!

Lady T. Dido shall make that good, or I will for her.
Here, Dido Wispe, there's for your Hannibal;
He is your countryman as well as valentine.

Wispe. Here, master Hannibal, my lady's bounty
For her poor woman, Wispe.

Pup. Brave Carthage queen!
And such was Dido: I will ever be
Champion to her, who Juno is to thee.

Dame T. Your ladyship is very welcome here.
Please you, good madam, to go near the house.

Lady T. Turfe's wife, I come thus far to seek your husband.
Having some business to impart unto him;
Is he at home?

Dame T. O no, an it shall please you:
He is posted hence to Pancridge, with a witness.
Young justice Bramble has kept level coyl
Here in our quarters, stole away our daughter,
And master Turfe's run after, as he can,
To stop the marriage, if it will be stopp'd.

Pol. Madam, these tidings are not much amiss:
For if the justice have the maid in keep,
You need not fear the marriage of your son.

Lady T. That somewhat easeth my suspicious breast.
Tell me, Turfe's wife, when was my son with Awdrey?
How long is it since you saw him at your house?

Pup. Dame, let me take this rump out of your mouth.

Dame T. What mean you by that, sir?

Pup. Rump and taile's all one,
But I would use a reverence for my lady:
I would not zay, sur-reverence, the tale
Out of your mouth, but rather take the rump.

Dame T. A well-bred youth! and vull of favour you are.

Pup. What might they zay, when I were gone, if I
Not weigh'd my words? This Puppy is a vool,
Great Hannibal's an ass; he hath no breeding:
No, lady gay, you shall not zay
That your Val. Puppy, was so unlucky,
In speech to fail, as to name a tail,
Be as be may be, 'vore a fair lady.

Lady T. Leave jesting; tell us when you saw our son.

Pup. Marry, it is two hours ago.

Lady T. Since you saw him?

Pup. You might have seen him too, if you had look'd up;
For it shined as bright as day.

Lady T. I mean my son.

Pup. Your sun, and our sun, are they not all one?

Lady T. Fool, thou mistak'st; I ask'd thee for my son.

Pup. I had thought there had been no more sons than one.
I know not what you ladies have, or may have.

Pol. Didst thou ne'er hear my lady had a son?

Pup. She may have twenty; but for a son, unless
She mean precisely, 'squire Tub, her zon,
He was here now, and brought my master word
That justice Bramble had got mistress Awdrey:
But whither he be gone, here's none can tell.

Lady T. Martin, I wonder at this strange discourse:
The fool, it seems, tells true; my son the 'squire
Was doubtless here this morning: for the match,
I'll smother what I think, and staying here,
Attend the sequel of this strange beginning. —
Turfe's wife, my people and I will trouble thee
Until we hear some tidings of thy husband;
The rather for my party-valentine. [*Exeunt.*

SCENE III

PANCRAS.

Enter TURFE, AWDREY, CLENCH, MEDLAY, PAN, and SCRIBEN.

Turfe. Well, I have carried it, and will triumph
Over this justice as becomes a constable,
And a high constable: next our St. George,
Who rescued the king's daughter, I will ride;
Above prince Arthur.

Clench. Or our Shoreditch duke.

Med. Or Pancridge earl.

Pan. Or Bevis, or sir Guy,
Who were high constables both.

Clench. One of Southampton —

Med. The t'other of Warwick-castle.

Turfe. You shall work it
Into a story for me, neighbour Medlay,
Over my chimney. Scri. I can give you, sir,
A Roman story of a petty-constable,
That had a daughter that was call'd Virginia,
Like mistress Awdrey, and as young as she;
And how her father bare him in the business,
'Gainst justice Appius, a decemvir in Rome,
And justice of assize.

Turfe. That, that, good D'ogenes!
A learned man is a chronicle. Scri. I can tell you
A thousand of great Pompey, Cæsar, Trajan,
All the high constables there.

Turfe. That was their place!
They were no more. Scri. Dictator and high constable
Were both the same.

Med. High constable was more though:
He laid Dick Tator by the heels.

Pan. Dick Toter!
He was one o' the waights o' the city, I have read o"un;
He was a fellow would be drunk, debauch'd —
And he did zet 'un in the stocks indeed:
His name was Vadian, and a cunning toter.

Awd. Was ever silly maid thus posted off,
That should have had three husbands in one day;
Yet, by bad fortune, am possest of none!
I went to church to have been wed to Clay,
Then 'squire Tub he seized me on the way,
And thought to have had me, but he mist his aim;
And justice Bramble, nearest of the three,
Was well-nigh married to me; when by chance,
In rush'd my father, and broke off that dance.

Turfe. Ay, girl, there's ne'er a justice on 'em all
Shall teach the constable to guard his own:
Let's back to Kentish-town, and there make merry:
These news will be glad tidings to my wife.
Thou shalt have Clay, my wench: that word shall stand.
He's found by this time, sure, or else he's drown'd;
The wedding-dinner will be spoil'd: make haste.

Awd. Husbands, they say, grow thick, but thin are sown;
I care not who it be, so I have one,

Turfe. Ay, zay you zo! perhaps you shall ha' none for that.

Awd. None, out upon me! what shall I do then?

Med. Sleep, mistress Awdrey, dream on proper men. [*Exeunt.*

SCENE IV

Another part of the same.

Enter Sir HUGH and PREAMBLE.

Hugh. O *bone Deus,* have you seen the like!
Here was, Hodge hold thine ear fair, whilst I strike.
Body o' me, how came this geer about?

Pre. I know not, Canon, but it falls out cross.
Nor can I make conjecture by the circumstance
Of these events; it was impossible,
Being so close and politicly carried,
To come so quickly to the ears of Turfe.
O priest! had but thy slow delivery
Been nimble, and thy lazy Latin tongue
But run the forms o'er with that swift dispatch
As had been requisite, all had been well.

Hugh. What should have been, that never loved the friar;
But thus you see the old adage verified,
Midta cadunt inter you can guess the rest,
Many things fall between the cup and lip;
And though they touch, you are not sure to drink.
You lack'd good fortune, we had done our parts:
Give a man fortune, throw him in the sea,
The properer man, the worse luck: stay a time;
Tempus edax — In time the stately ox, —
Good counsels lightly never come too late.

Pre. You, sir, will run your counsels out of breath.

Hugh. Spur a free horse, he'll run himself to death.
Sancti Evangelista;! here comes Miles!

Enter METAPHOR.

Pre. What news, man, with our new-made pursuivant?

Met. A pursuiyant! would I were — or more pursie,
And had more store of money; or less pursie,
And had more store of breath: you call me pursuivant,
But I could never vaunt of any purse
I had, sin' you were my godfathers and godmothers,
And gave me that nick-name.

Pre. What's now the matter?

Met. Nay, 'tis no matter, I have been simply beaten.

Hugh. What is become of the 'squire and thy prisoner *t*

Met. The lines of blood run streaming from my head,
Can speak what rule the 'squire hath kept with me.

Pre. I pray thee, Miles, relate the manner how.

Met. Be't known unto you by these presents then,
That I, Miles Metaphor, your worship's clerk,
Have e'en been beaten to an allegory,
By multitude of hands. Had they been but
Some five or six, I had whipp'd them all, like tops
In Lent, and hurl'd them into Hobler's hole,
Or the next ditch; I had crack'd all their costards,
As nimbly as a squirrel will crack nuts,
And flourished like to Hercules the porter
Among the pages. But when they came on
Like bees about a hive, crows about carrion,
Flies about sweetmeats; nay, like watermen
About a fare: then was poor Metaphor
Glad to give up the honour of the day,
To quit his charge to them, and run away
To save his life, only to tell this news.

Hugh. How indirectly all things are fallen out!
I cannot choose but wonder what they were
Rescued your rival from the keep of Miles;
But most of all, I cannot well digest
The manner how our purpose came to Turfe.

Pre. Miles, I will see that all thy hurts be drest.
As for the 'squire's escape, it matters not,
We have by this means disappointed him;
And that was all the main I aimed at.
But canon Hugh, now muster up thy wits,
And call thy thoughts into the consistory,
Search all the secret corners of thy cap,
To find another quaint devised drift.
To disappoint her marriage with this Clay:
Do that, and I'll reward thee jovially.

Hugh. Well said, magister justice. If I fit you not
With such a new and well-laid stratagem,
As never yet your ears did hear a finer,
Call me with Lilly, Bos, Fur, Sus aique Sacerdos.

Pre. I hear there's comfort in thy words yet. Canon.
I'll trust thy regulars, and say no more. *[Exeunt Hugh and Pre.*

Met. I'll follow too. And if the dapper priest
Be but as cunning, point in his device,
As I was in my lie, my master Bramble
Will stalk, as led by the nose with these new promises,
And fatted with supposes of fine hopes. *[Exit.*

SCENE V

Kentish-Town. — Before TURFE'S House.

Enter TURFE, Dame TURFE, Lady TUB, POL MARTIN, AWDREY, and PUPPY.

Turfe. Well, madam, I may thank the 'squire your son;
  For, but for him, I had been over-reach'-d.

Dame T. Now heaven's blessing light upon his heart!
  We are beholden to him, indeed, madam.

Lady T. But can you not resolve me where he is,
  Nor about what his purposes were bent?

Turfe. Madam, they no whit were concerning me,
  And therefore was I less inquisitive.

Lady T. Fair maid, in faith, speak truth, and not dissemble?
  Does he not often come and visit you?

Awd. His worship now and then, please you, takes pains
  To see my father and mother; but, for me,
  I know myself too mean for his high thoughts
  To stoop at, more than asking a light question,
  To make him merry, or to pass his time.

Lady T. A sober maid! call for my woman, Martin.

Pol. The maids and her half-valentine have plied her
With courtesy of the bride-cake and the bowl,
As she is laid awhile.

Lady T. O let her rest.
We will cross o'er to Canbury in the interim,
And so make home. — Farewell, good Turfe, and thy wife;
I wish your daughter joy. *[Exeunt Lady T. and Pol.*

Turfe. Thanks to your ladyship. —
Where is John Clay now, have you seen him yet?

Dame T. No, he has hid himself out of the way,
For fear of the hue and cry.

Turfe. What, walks that shadow
Avore 'un still? — Puppy, go seek 'un out,
Search all the corners that he haunts unto,
And call 'un forth. We'll once more to the church,
And try our vortunes: luck, son Valentine!
Where are the wise men all of Finsbury?

Pup. Where wise men should be; at the ale and bride-cake.
I would this couple had their destiny,
Or to be hang'd, or married out o' the way:

Enter CLENCH, MEDLAY, SCRIBEN, etc..

Man cannot get the mount'nance of an egg-shell
To stay his stomach. Vaith, for mine own part,
I have zupp'd up so much broth as would have cover'd
A leg o' beef o'er head and ears in the porridge-pot,
And yet I cannot sussifie wild nature.
Would they were once dispatch'd, we might to dinner.
I am with child of a huge stomach, and long,
Till by some honest midwife piece of beef
I be deliver'd of it: I must go now
And hunt out for this Kilborn calf, John Clay,
Whom where to find, I know not, nor which way. *[Exit.*

Enter Sir HUGH, disguised as a captain.

Hugh. Thus as a beggar in a king's disguise,
Or an old cross well sided with a may-pole,
Comes canon Hugh accoutred as you see.
Disguised, soldado-like. Mark his device:
The canon is that captain Thums was robb'd,
These bloody scars upon my face are wounds,
This scarf upon mine arm shews my late hurts,
And thus am I to gull the constable.
Now have among you for a man at arms! *[Aside.*
Friends, by your leave, which of you is one Turfe?

Turfe. Sir, I am Turfe, if you would speak with me.

Hugh. With thee, Turfe, if thou be'st high constable.

Turfe. I am both Turfe, sir, and high constable.

Hugh. Then, Turfe or Scurfe, high or low constable,
Know, I was once a captain at St. Quintin's,
And passing cross the ways over the country,
This morning, betwixt this and Hampstead-heath,
Was by a crew of clowns robb'd, bobb'd and hurt.
No sooner had I got my wounds bound up,
But with much pain I went to the next justice,
One master Bramble, here at Maribone:
And here a warrant is, which he hath directed
For you, one Turfe, if your name be Toby Turfe,
Who have let fall, they say, the hue and cry;
And you shall answer it afore the justice.

Turfe. Heaven and hell, dogs and devils, what is this!
Neighbours, was ever constable thus cross'd?
What shall we do?

Med. Faith, all go hang ourselves;
I know no other way to escape the law.

Re-enter PUPPY.

Pup. News, news, O news —

Turfe. What, hast thou found out Clay?

Pup. No, sir, the news is, that I cannot find him.

Hugh. Why do you dally, you damn'd russet-coat?
You peasant, nay, you clown, you constable!
See that you bring forth the suspected party,
Or by mine honour, which I won in field,
I'll make you pay for it afore the justice.

Turfe. Fie, fie! O wife, I'm now in a fine pickle.
He that was most suspected is not found;
And which now makes me think he did the deed,
He thus absents him, and dares not be seen.
Captain, my innocence will plead for me.
Wife, I must go, needs, whom the devil drives:
Pray for me, wife and daughter, pray for me.

Hugh. I'll lead the way — thus is the match put off, —
And if my plot succeed, as I have laid it,
My captainship shall cost him many a crown.
[*Aside. Exeunt all but Dame T., Awd., and Puppy.*

Dame T. So, we have brought our eggs to a fair market.
Out on that villain Clay! would he do a robbery?
I'll ne'er trust smooth-faced tileman for his sake.

Awd. Mother, the still sow eats up all the draff.
[Exeunt Dame T. and Awd.

Pup. Thus is my master, Toby Turfe, the pattern
Of all the painful adventures now in print!
I never could hope better of this match,
This bride-ale; for the night before to-day,
(Which is within man's memory, I take it,)
At the report of it an ox did speak,
Who died soon after; a cow lost her calf;
The bell-weather was flay'd for't; a fat hog
Was singed, and wash'd, and shaven all over, to
Look ugly 'gainst this day: the ducks they quack'd,
The hens too cackled; at the noise whereof
A drake was seen to dance a headless round;
The goose was cut in the head to hear it too:
Brave chant-it-clear, his noble heart was done,
His comb was cut; and two or three of his wives
Or fairest concubines, had their necks broke
Ere they would zee this day: to mark the verven
Heart of a beast! the very pig, the pig
This very morning, as he was a roasting,
Cried out his eyes, and made a shew, as he would
Have bit in two the spit; as he would say,
There shall no roast-meat be this dismal day.
And zure, I think, if I had not got his tongue
Between my teeth and eat it, he had spoke it.
Well, I will in and cry too; never leave
Crying until our maids may drive a buck
With my salt tears at the next washing-day. *[Exit.*

ACT IV

SCENE I

Maribone. – A Room in Justice PREAMBLE'S House.

Enter Justice PREAMBLE, Sir HUGH, disguised as before, TURFE, and METAPHOR.

Pre. Keep out those fellows; I'll have none come in
But the high constable, the man of peace,
And the queen's captain, the brave man of war.
Now, neighbour Turfe, the cause why you are call'd
Before me by my warrant, but unspecified,
Is this; and pray you mark it thoroughly.
Here is a gentleman, and, as it seems,
Both of good birth, fair speech, and peaceable;
Who was this morning robb'd here in the wood:
You, for your part, a man of good report,
Of credit, landed, and of fair demeans,
And by authority, high constable;
Are, notwithstanding, touch'd in this complaint,
Of being careless in the hue and cry.
I cannot choose but grieve a soldier's loss;
And I am sorry too for your neglect,
Being my neighbour: this is all I object.

Hugh. This is not all; I can allege far more,
And almost urge him for an accessary.
Good master justice, give me leave to speak,
For I am plaintiff: let not neighbourhood
Make him secure, or stand on privilege.

Pre. Sir, I dare use no partiality;
Object then what you please, so it be truth.

Hugh. This more, and which is more than he can answer;
Besides his letting fall the hue and cry,
He doth protect the man charged with the felony,
And keeps him hid, I hear, within his house,
Because he is affied unto his daughter.

Turfe. I do defy 'un, so shall she do too.
I pray your worship's favour let me have hearing.
I do convess, 'twas told me such a velony,
And't not disgrieved me a little, when 'twas told me,
Vor I was going to church to marry Awdrey:
And who should marry her but this very Clay,
Who was charged to be the chief thief o"em all.
Now I (the halter stick me if I tell
Your worships any leazins) did fore-think 'un
The truest man, till he waz run away:
I thought I had had 'un as zure as in a zaw-pit,
Or in mine oven; nay, in the town-pound:
I was zo zure o"un, I'd have gi'n my life for 'un,
Till he did start: but now I zee 'un guilty,
Az var as I can look at 'un. Would you ha' more?

Hugh. Yes, I will have, sir, what the law will give me.
You gave your word to see him safe forth-coming;
I challenge that: but that is forfeited;
Beside, your carelessness in the pursuit,
Argues your slackness and neglect of duty,
Which ought be punish'd with severity.

Pre. He speaks but reason, Turfe. Bring forth the man
And you are quit; but otherwise, your word
Binds you to make amends for all his loss,
And think yourself befriended, if he take it
Without a farther suit or going to law.
Come to a composition with him, Turfe,
The law is costly, and will draw on charge.

Turfe. Yes, I do know, I vurst mun vee a returney,
And then make legs to my great man o' law,
To be o' my counsel, and take trouble-vees,
And yet zay nothing for me, but devise
All district means, to ransackle me o' my money.
A pest'lence prick the throats o"em! I do know 'em,
As well az I waz in their bellies, and brought up there.
What would you ha' me do, what would you ask of me?

Hugh. I ask the restitution of my money,
And will not bate one penny of the sum;
Fourscore and five pound: and I ask, besides,
Amendment for my hurts; my pain and suffering
Are loss enough for me, sir, to sit down with.
I'll put it to your worship; what you award me,
I'll take, and give him a general release.

Pre. And what say you now, neighbour Turfe?

Turfe. I put it
Even to your worship's bitterment, hab, nab.
I shall have a chance o' the dice for't, I hope, let 'em e'en run:
and —

Pre. Faith, then I'll pray you, 'cause he is my neighbour,
To take a hundred pound, and give him day.

Hugh. Saint Valentine's day, I will, this very day,
Before sun-set; my bond is forfeit else.

Turfe. Where will you have it paid?

Hugh. Faith, I am a stranger
Here in the country; know you canon Hugh,
The vicar of Paneras?

Turfe. Yes, who [knows] not him?

Hugh. I'll make him my attorney to receive it,
And give you a discharge.

Turfe. Whom shall I send for't?

Pre. Why, if you please, send Metaphor my clerk:
And, Turfe, I much commend thy willingness;
It's argument of thy integrity.

Turfe. But my integrity shall be my zelf still:
Good master Metaphor, give my wife this key,
And do but whisper it into her hand;
She knows it well enough; bid her, by that,
Deliver you the two zeal'd bags of silver,
That lie in the corner of the cupboard, stands
At my bed-side, they are vifty pound a piece;
And bring them to your master.

Met. If I prove not
As just a carrier as my friend Tom Long was,
Then call me his curtal; change my name of Miles,
To Guiles, Wiles, Piles, Biles, or the foulest name
You can devise, to crambo with for ale.
Hugh, [*takes Met aside.*] Come hither, Miles; bring by that token too
Fair Awdrey; say, her father sent for her.
Say, Clay is found, and waits at Pancras-church,
Where I attend to marry them in haste:
For, by this means, Miles, I may say't to thee,
Thy master must to Awdrey married be.
But not a word but mum: go, get thee gone,
Be wary of thy charge, and keep it close.

Met. O super-dainty canon, vicar incony!
Make no delay, Miles, but away;
And bring the wench and money. [*Exit.*

Hugh. Now, sir, I see you meant but honestly:
And, but that business calls me hence away,
I would not leave you till the sun were lower. —
But, master justice, one word, sir, with you. [*Aside to Pre.*
By the same token, is your mistress sent for
By Metaphor, your clerk, as from her father;
Who, when she comes, I'll marry her to you,
Unwitting to this Turfe, who shall attend
Me at the parsonage: this was my plot,
Which I must now make good, turn canon again,
In my square cap. I humbly take my leave. [*Exit.*

Pre. Adieu, good captain. — Trust me, neighbour Turfe,
He seems to be a sober gentleman:
But this distress hath somewhat stirr'd his patience.
And men, you know, in such extremities,
Apt not themselves to points of courtesy;
I'm glad you have made this end.

Turfe. You stood my friend,
I thank your justice-worship; pray you be
Prezent anon at tendering of the money,
And zee me have a discharge; vor I have no craft
In your law quiblins.

Pre. I'll secure you, neighbour. *[Exeunt.*

SCENE II

The Country near MARIBONE.

Enter MEDLAY, CLENCH, PAN, and SCRIBEN.

Med. Indeed there is a woundy luck in names, sirs,
And a vain mystery, an a man knew where
To vind it. My godsire's name, I'll tell you,
Was In-and-In Shittle, and a weaver he was,
And it did fit his craft: for so his shittle
Went in and in still; this way, and then that way.
And he named me In-and-In Medlay; which serves
A joiner's craft, because that we do lay
Things in and in, in our work. But I am truly
Architectonicus professor, rather;
That is, as one would zay, an architect.

Clench. As I am a varrier and a visicary;
Horse-smith of Hamstead, and the whole town leach.

Med. Yes, you have done woundy cures, gossip Clench.

Clench. An I can zee the stale once through a urine-hole,
I'll give a shrewd guess, be it man or beast.
I cured an ale-wife once that had the staggers
Worse than five horses, without rowelling.
My god-phere was a Rabian or a Jew,
(You can tell, D'oge,) they call'd 'un doctor Rasi. *Scri.* One
Rasis was a great Arabic doctor.

Clench. He was king Harry's doctor, and my god-phere.

Pan. Mine was a merry Greek, To-Pan of Twiford,
A jovial tinker, and a stopper of holes;
Who left me metal-man of Belsise, his heir.

Med. But what was yours, D'oge? *Scri.* Vaith, I cannot tell,
If mine were kyrsin'd or no: but zure he had
A kyrsin name, that he left me, Diogenes.
A mighty learned man, but pestilence poor;
Vor he had no house, save an old tub, to dwell in,
(I vind that in records,) and still he turn'd it
In the wind's teeth, as't blew on his backside,
And there they would lie routing one at other,
A week sometimes.

Med. Thence came, A Tale of a Tub,
And the virst *Tale of a Tub*, old D'ogenes' Tub. *Scri.* That was
avore sir Peter Tub or his lady.

Pan. Ay, or the 'squire their son, Tripoly Tub.

Clench. The 'squire is a fine gentleman.

Med. He is more,
A gentleman and a half; almost a knight,
Within zix inches; that is his true measure.

Clench. Zure you can gage 'un.

Med. To a streak, or less;
I know his d'ameters and circumference:
A knight is six diameters, and a 'squire
Is vive, and zomewhat more; I know't by compass
And scale of man. I have upon my rule here
The just perportions of a knight, a 'squire;
With a tame justice, or an officer rampant,
Upon the bench, from the high constable
Down to the headborough, or tithing-man,
Or meanest minister of the peace, God save 'un!

Pan. Why you can tell us by the 'squire, neighbour,
Whence he is call'd a constable, and whafiore.

Med. No, that's a book-case: Scriben can do that.
That's writing and reading, and records. Scri. Two words,
Cyning and staple, make a constable;
As we would say, a hold or stay for the king.

Clench. All constables are truly Johns for the king,
Whate'er their names are, be they Tony or Roger.

Med. And all are sworn as vingars o' the one hand,
To hold together 'gainst the breach o' the peace;
The high constable is the thumb, as one would zay,
The hold-fast o' the rest.

Pan. Pray luck he speed
Well in the business between captain Thums
And him!

Med. I'll warrant 'un for a groat;
I have his measures here in rithmetique,
How he should hear 'un self in all the lines
Of's place and office: let us zeek'un out. *[Exeunt.*

SCENE III

The Country near KENTISH-TOWN.

Enter TUB and HILTS.

Tub. Hilts, how dost thou like of this our good day's work?

Hilts. As good e'en ne'er a whit, as ne'er the better.

Tub. Shall we to Pancridge or to Kentish-town, Hilts?

Hilts. Let Kentish-town or Pancridge come to us,
If either will: I will go home again.

Tub. Faith, Basket, our success hath been but bad,
And nothing prospers that we undertake;
For we can neither meet with Clay nor Awdrey,
The canon Hugh, nor Turfe the constable:
We are like men that wander in strange woods,
And lose ourselves in search of them we seek.

Hilts. This was because we rose on the wrong side;
But as I am now here, just in the mid-way,
I'll zet my sword on the pummel, and that line
The point vails to, we'll take, whether it be
To Kentish-town, the church, or home again.

Tub. Stay, stay thy hand: here's justice Bramble's clerk,

Enter METAPHOR.

The unlucky hare hath crossed us all this day.
I'll stand aside whilst thou pump'st out of him
His business, Hilts; and how he's now employed. *[Walks aside.*

Hilts. Let me alone, I'll use him in this kind.

Met. Oh for a pad-horse, pack-horse, or a post-horse,
To bear me on his neck, his back, or his croup!
I am as weary with running as a mill-horse
That hath led the mill once, twice, thrice about,
After the breath hath been out of his body.
I could get up upon a pannier, a pannel,
Or, to say truth, a very pack-saddle,
Till all my honey were turn'd into gall,
And I could sit in the seat no longer: —
Oh [for] the legs of a lackey now, or a footman,
Who is the surbater of a clerk currant,
And the confounder of his trestles dormant!
But who have we here, just in the nick?

Hilts. I am neither nick, nor in the nick; therefore
You lie, sir Metaphor.

Met. Lie! how?

Hilts. Lie so, sir. *[Strikes up his heels.*

Met. I lie not yet in my throat.

Hills. Thou liest on the ground.
Dost thou know me?

Met. Yes, I did know you too late.

Hilts. What is my name, then?

Met. Basket.

Hilts. Basket what?

Met. Basket the great —

Hilts. The great what?

Met. Lubber —
I should say, lover, of the 'squire his master.

Hilts. Great is my patience, to forbear thee thus,
Thou scrape-hill scoundrel, and thou scum of man;
Uncivil, orange-tawney-coated clerk!
Thou cam'st but half a thing into the world,
And wast made up of patches, parings, shreds:
Thou, that when last thou wert put out of service,
Travell'dst to Hamstead-heath on an Ash-We'nesday,
Where thou didst stand six weeks the Jack of Lent,
For boys to hurl, three throws a penny, at thee,
To make thee a purse: seest thou this bold bright blade?
This sword shall shred thee as small unto the grave,
As minced meat for a pye. I'll set thee in earth
All, save thy head and thy right arm at liberty,
To keep thy hat off while I question thee
What, why, and whither thou wert going now,
With a face ready to break out with business?
And tell me truly, lest I dash't in pieces.

Met. Then, Basket, put thy smiter up, and hear;
I dare not tell the truth to a drawn sword.
Hilts. 'Tis sheath'd; stand up, speak without fear or wit.

Met. [*me?.*] I know not what they mean; but constable Turfe
    Sends here his key for monies in his cupboard,
    Which he must pay the captain that was robb'd
      This morning. Smell you nothing?

          Hilts. No, not I;
      Thy breeches yet are honest.

          Met. As my mouth.
    Do you not smell a rat? I tell you truth,
I think all's knavery; for the canon whisper'd
Me in the ear, when Turfe had gi'n me his key,
By the same token to bring mistress Awdrey,
    As sent for thither; and to say, John Clay
Is found, which is indeed to get the wench
Forth for my master, who is to be married
When she comes there: the canon has his rules
    Ready, and all there, to dispatch the matter.

Tub. [*comes forward.*] Now, on my life, this is the canon's plot.
              —
    Miles, I have heard all thy discourse to Basket.
    Wilt thou be true, and I'll reward thee well,
    To make me happy in my mistress Awdrey?

Met. Your worship shall dispose of Metaphor,
Through all his parts, e'en from the sole of the head
To the crown of the foot, to manage of your service.

Tub. Then do thy message to the mistress Turfe,
    Tell her thy token, bring the money hither,
    And likewise take young Awdrey to thy charge;
    Which done, here, Metaphor, we will attend,
        And intercept thee: and for thy reward
        You two shall share the money, I the maid;
        If any take offence, I'll make all good.

Met. But shall I have half the money, sir, in faith?

Tub. Ay, on my 'squireship shalt thou, and my land.

Met. Then, if I make not, sir, the cleanliest 'scuse
    To get her hither, and be then as careful
    To keep her for you, as 'twere for myself.
    Down on your knees, and pray that honest Miles
    May break his neck ere he get o'er two stiles.

Tub. Make haste, then; we will wait here thy return. [*Exit Met.*
    This luck unlook'd for hath reviv'd my hopes,
    Which were opprest with a dark melancholy:
        In happy time we linger'd on the way,
        To meet these summons of a better sound,
        Which are the essence of my soul's content.

Hilts. This heartless fellow, shame to serving-men,
    Stain of all liveries, what fear makes him do!
    How sordid, wretched and unworthy things!
        Betray his master's secrets, ope the closet
        Of his devices, force the foolish justice
    Make way for your love, plotting of his own;
    Like him that digs a trap to catch another,
        And falls into't himself!

Tub. So would I have it,
And hope 'twill prove a jest to twit the justice with.

Hilts. But that this poor white-liver'd rogue should do it,
And merely out of fear!

Tub. And hope of money, Hilts:
A valiant man will nibble at that bait.

Hilts. Who, but a fool, will refuse money proffer'd Î

Tub. And sent by so good chance? Pray heaven he speed.

Hilts. If he come empty-handed, let him count
To go back empty-headed; I'll not leave him
So much of brain in's pate, with pepper and vinegar,
To be serv'd in for sauce to a calf's head.

Tub. Thou [wilt] serve him rightly, Hilts.

Hilts. I'll seal [to] as much
With my hand, as I dare say now with my tongue.
But if you get the lass from Dargison,
What will you do with her Î

Tub. We'll think of that
When once we have her in possession, governor. [*Exeunt.*

SCENE IV

Another Part of the same.

Enter PUPPY, and METAPHOR with AUDREY.

Pup. You see we trust you, master Metaphor,
With mistress Awdrey; pray you use her well,
As a gentlewoman should be used. For my part,
I do incline a little to the serving-man;
We have been of a coat — I had one like yours;
Till it did play me such a sleeveless errand,
As I had nothing where to put mine arms in,
And then I threw it off. Pray you go before her,
Serving-man-like, and see that your nose drop not.
As for example, you shall see me: mark,
How I go afore her! so do you, sweet Miles.
She for her own part is a woman cares not
What man can do unto her in the way
Of honesty and good manners: so farewell,
Fair mistress Awdrey; farewell, master Miles.
I have brought you thus far onward o' your way:
I must go back now to make clean the rooms.
Where my good lady has been. Pray you commend me
To bridegroom Clay, and bid him bear up stiff.

Met. Thank you, good Hannibal Puppy; I shall fit
The leg of your commands with the strait buskins
Of dispatch presently.

Pup. Farewell, fine Metaphor. [*Exit.*

Met. Come, gentle mistress, will you please to walk?

Awd. I love not to be led; I would go alone.

Met. Let not the mouse of my good meaning, lady,
Be snapp'd up in the trap of your suspicion,
To lose the tail there, either of her truth,
Or swallow'd by the cat of misconstruction.

Awd. You are too finical for me; speak plain, sir.

Enter Tub and Hilts.

Tub. Welcome again, my Awdrey, welcome, love!
You shall with me; in faith deny me not:
I cannot brook the second hazard, mistress.

Awd. Forbear, 'squire Tub, as mine own mother says,
I am not for your mowing: you'll be flown
Ere I be fledge.

Hilts. Hast thou the money, Miles?

Met. Here are two bags, there's fifty pound in each.

Tub. Nay, Awdrey, I possess you for this time —
Sirs, take that coin between you, and divide it.
My pretty sweeting, give me now the leave
To challenge love and marriage at your hands.

Awd. Now, out upon you, are you not asham'd!
What will my lady say? In faith, I think
She was at our house, and I think she ask'd for you;
And I think she hit me in the teeth with you,
I thank her ladyship: and I think she means
Not to go hence till she has found you.

Tub. How say you!
Was then my lady mother at your house?
Let's have a word aside.

Awd. Yes, twenty words. [*They walk aside.*

Enter Lady TUB and POL MABTIN.

Lady T. 'Tis strange, a motion, but I know not what,
Comes in my mind, to leave the way to Totten,
And turn to Kentish-town again my journey —
And see! my son, Pol Martin, with his Awdrey!
Erewhile we left her at her father's house,
And hath he thence removed her in such haste!
What shall I do, shall I speak fair, or chide?

Pol. Madam, your worthy son with duteous care
Can govern his affections; rather then,
Break off their conference some other way,
Pretending ignorance of what you know.

Tub. An this be all, fair Awdrey, I am thine.

Lady T. [*comes forward.*] Mine you were once, though scarcely
now your own.
Hilts. 'Slid, my lady, my lady!

Met. Is this my lady bright? [*Exit.*

Tub. Madam, you took me now a little tardy.

Lady T. At prayers I think you were: what, so devout
Of late, that you will shrive you to all confessors
You meet by chance! come, go with me, good 'squire,
And leave your linen: I have now a business,
And of importance, to impart unto you.

Tub. Madam, I pray you spare me but an hour:
Please you to walk before, I follow you.

Lady T. It must be now, my business lies this way.

Tub. Will not an hour hence, madam, excuse me?

Lady T. 'Squire, these excuses argue more your guilt.
You have some new device now to project,
Which the poor tileman scarce will thank you for.
What! will you go?

Tub. I have ta'en a charge upon me,
To see this maid conducted to her father,
Who, with the canon Hugh, stays her at Paneras,
To see her married to the same John Clay.

Lady T. 'Tis very well; but, 'squire, take you no care,
I'll send Pol Martin with her for that office:
You shall along with me; it is decreed.

Tub. I have a little business with a friend, madam.

Lady T. That friend shall stay for you, or you for him. —
Pol Martin, take the maiden to your care;
Commend me to her father.

Tub. I will follow you.

Lady T. Tut, tell not me of following.

Tub. I'll but speak
A word.

Lady T. No whispering; you forget yourself,
And make your love too palpable: a 'squire,
And think so meanly! fall upon a cowshard!
You know my mind. Come, I will to Turfe's house,
And see for Dido and our Valentine. —
Pol Martin, look to your charge, I'll look to mine.
[Exeunt Lady T., Tub, and Hilts.

Pol. I smile to think, after so many proffers
This maid hath had, she now should fall to me,
That I should have her in my custody!
'Twere but a mad trick to make the essay,
And jump a match with her immediately.
She's fair and handsome, and she's rich enough;
Both time and place minister fair occasion:
Have at it then! *[Aside.]* — Fair lady, can you love?

Awd. No, sir; what's that?

Pol. A toy which women use.

Awd. If it be a toy, it's good to play withal.

Pol. We will not stand discoursing of the toy;
The way is short, please you to prove it, mistress.

Awd. If you do mean to stand so long upon it,
 I pray you let me give it a short cut, sir.

Pol. It's thus, fair maid: are you disposed to marry?

Awd. You are disposed to ask.

Pol. Are you to grant?

Awd. Nay, now I see you are disposed indeed.

Pol. I see the wench wants but a little wit,
And that defect her wealth may well supply:
In plain terms, tell me, will you have me, Awdrey?

Awd. In as plain terms, I tell you who would have me,
John Clay would have me, but he hath too hard hands,
 I like not him; besides, he is a thief.
And justice Bramble, he would fain have catch'd me:
But the young 'squire, he rather than his life,
Would have me yet; and make me a lady, he says,
And be my knight to do me true knight's service,
Before his lady mother. Can you make me
 A lady, would I have you?

Pol. I can give you
A silken gown and a rich petticoat,
And a French hood. — All fools love to be brave:
I find her humour, and I will pursue it. *[Aside. Exeunt.*

SCENE V

KENTISH-TOWN.

Enter Lady TUB, Dame TURFE, Squire TUB, and HILTS.

Lady T. And, as I told thee, she was intercepted
By the 'squire, here, my son, and this bold ruffian,
His man, who safely would have carried her
Unto her father, and the canon Hugh;
But for more care of the security,
My huisher hath her now in his grave charge.

Dame T. Now on my faith and holydom, we are
Beholden to your worship. She's a girl,
A foolish girl, and soon may tempted be;
But if this day pass well once o'er her head,
I'll wish her trust to herself: for I have been
A very mother to her, though I say it.

Tub. Madam, 'tis late, and Pancridge is in your way;
I think your ladyship forgets yourself.

Lady T. Your mind runs much on Pancridge. Well, young 'squire,
The black ox never trod yet on your foot;
These idle phant'sies will forsake you one day.
Come, mistress Turfe, will you go take a walk
Over the fields to Pancridge, to your husband?

Dame T. Madam, I had been there an hour ago,
   But that I waited on my man, Ball Puppy. —
   What, Ball, I say! — I think the idle slouch
   Be fallen asleep in the barn, he stays so long.

Enter PUPPY hastily from the barn.

Pup. Sattin, in the name of velvet-sattin, dame!
   The devil, O the devil is in the barn!
   Help, help! a legion [of] spirits, [a] legion,
      Is in the barn! in every straw a devil!

Dame T. Why dost thou bawl so, Puppy? speak, what ails thee?

Pup. My name's Ball Puppy, I have seen the devil
   Among the straw. O for a cross! a collop
      Of friar Bacon, or a conjuring stick
   Of doctor Faustus! spirits are in the barn.

Tub. How, spirits in the barn! — Basket, go see.

Hilts. Sir, an you were my master ten times over,
   And 'squire to boot; I know, and you shall pardon me:
   Send me 'mong devils! I zee you love me not.
   Hell be at their game; I will not trouble them.

Tub. Go see; I warrant thee there's no such matter.

Hilts. An they were giants, 'twere another matter,
   But devils! no, if I be torn in pieces,
   What is your warrant worth? I'll see the fiend
      Set fire o' the barn, ere I come there.

Dame T. Now all zaints bless us, and if he be there,
He is an ugly spright, I warrant.

Pup. As ever
Held flesh-hook, dame, or handled fire-fork rather,
They have put me in a sweet pickle, dame;
But that my lady Valentine smells of musk,
I should be ashamed to press into this presence.

Lady T. Basket, I pray thee see what is the miracle.

Tub. Come, go with me; I'll lead. Why stand'st thou, man?

Hilts. Cock's precious, master, you are not mad indeed.
You will not go to hell before your time?

Tub. Why art thou thus afraid?

Hilts. No, not afraid?
But, by your leave, I'll come no nearer the barn.

Dame T. Puppy, wilt thou go with me?

Pup. How, go with you!
Whither, into the barn? to whom, the devil?
Or to do what there? to be torn amongst 'um!
Stay for my master, the high constable,
Or In-and-In the headborough; let them go
Into the barn with warrant, seize the fiend,
And set him in the stocks for his ill rule:
'Tis not for me that am but flesh and blood,
To meddle with 'un; vor I cannot, nor I wu' not.

Lady T. I pray thee, Tripoly, look what is the matter.

Tub. That shall I, madam. [*Goes into the barn.*

Hilts. Heaven protect my master!
I tremble every joint till he be back.

Pup. Now, now, even now, they are tearing him in pieces;
Now are they tossing of his legs and arms,
Like loggets at a pear-tree; I'll to the hole,
Peep in, and look whether he lives or dies.

Hilts. I would not be in my master's coat for thousands.

Pup. Then pluck it off, and turn thyself away.
O the devil, the devil, the devil!

Hilts. Where, man, where?

Dame T. Alas, that ever we were born! So near too?

Pup. The 'squire hath him in his hand, and leads him
Out by the collar.

Re-enter TUB, dragging in CLAY.

Dame T. O this is John Clay.

Lady T. John Clay at Paneras, is there to be married.

Tub. This was the spirit revell'd in the barn.

Pup. The devil he was! was this he was crawling
Among the wheat-straw? had it been the barley,
I should have ta'en him for the devil in drink;
The spirit of the bride-ale: but poor John,
Tame John of Clay, that sticks about the bung-hole —

Hilts. If this be all your devil, I would take
In hand to conjure him: but hell take me,
If e'er I come in a right devil's walk,
If I can keep me out on't.

Tub. Well meant, Hilts. *[Exit.*

Lady T. But how came Clay thus hid here in the straw,
When news was brought to you all he was at Pancridge,
And you believed it?

Dame T. Justice Bramble's man
Told me so, madam; and by that same token,
And other things, he had away my daughter,
And two seal'd bags of money.

Lady T. Where's the 'squire,
Is he gone hence?

Dame T. He was here, madam, but now.

Clay. Is the hue and cry past by?

Pup. Ay, ay, John Clay.

Clay. And am I out of danger to be hang'd?

Pup. Hang'd, John! yes, sure; unless, as with the proverb,
You mean to make the choice of your own gallows.

Clay. Nay, then all's well: hearing your news, Ball Puppy
You brought from Paddington, I e'en stole home here,
And thought to hide me in the barn e'er since.

Pup. O wonderful! and news was brought us here,
  You were at Pancridge, ready to be married.

Clay. No, faith, I ne'er was further than the barn.

Dame T. Haste, Puppy, call forth mistress Dido Wispe,
  My lady's gentlewoman, to her lady;
  And call yourself forth, and a couple of maids,
  To wait upon me: we are all undone,
  My lady is undone, her fine young son,
    The 'squire, is got away.

Lady T. Haste, haste, good Valentine.

Dame T. And you, John Clay, you are undone too! all!
  My husband is undone by a true key,
  But a false token; and myself's undone,
  By parting with my daughter, who'll be married
To somebody that she should not, if we haste not. *[Exeunt.*

ACT V

SCENE I

The Fields near KENTISH-TOWN.

Enter Squire TUB and POL MARTIN.

Tub. I pray thee, good Pol Martin, shew thy diligence,
And faith in both; get her, but so disguised
The canon may not know her, and leave me
To plot the rest: I will expect thee here. *[Exit.*

Pol. You shall, 'squire. I'll perform it with all care,
If all my lady's wardrobe will disguise her. —
Come, mistress Awdrey.

Enter AWDBEY.

Awd. Is the 'squire gone?

Pol. He'll meet us by and by, where he appointed;
You shall be brave anon, as none shall know you. *[Exeunt.*

SCENE II

Kentish-Town.

Enter Clench, Medlay, Pan, and Scriben.

Clench. I wonder where the queen's high constable is,
I vear they ha' made 'un away.

Med. No zure; the justice
Dare not conzent to that: he'll zee 'un forth-coming.

Pan. He must, vor we can all take corpulent oath
We zaw 'un go in there. Scri. Ay, upon record:
The clock dropt twelve at Maribone.

Med. You are right, D'oge,
Zet down to a minute; now 'tis a' most vowre.

Clench. Here comes 'squire Tub. Scri. And's governor, master
Basket —

Enter TUB and HILTS.

Hilts; do you know'un? a valiant wise fellow.
As tall a man on his hands as goes on veet!
Bless you, mass' Basket.

Hilts. Thank you, good D'oge.

Tub. Who's that?

Hilts. D'oge Scriben the great writer, sir, of Chalcot.

Tub. And who the rest?

Hilts. The wisest heads o' the hundred.
Medlay the joiner, headborough of Islington,
Pan of Belsise, and Clench the leach of Hamstead,
The high constable's counsel here of Finsbury.

Tub. Present me to them, Hilts, 'squire Tub of Totten.

Hilts. Wise men of Finsbury, make place for a 'squire,
I bring to your acquaintance, Tub of Totten.
'Squire Tub, my master, loves all men of virtue,
And longs, as one would zay, till he be one o' you.

Clench. His worship's welcum to our company:
Would it were wiser for 'un!

Pan. Here be some on us
Are call'd the witty men over a hundred. Scri. And zome a
thousand, when the muster-day comes.

Tub. I long, as my man Hilts said, and my governor,
To be adopt in your society.
Can any man make a masque here in this company?

Pan. A masque! what's that? Scri. A mumming or a show,
With vizards and fine clothes.

Clench. A disguise, neighbour,
Is the true word: There stands the man can do't, sir;
Medlay the joiner, In-and-in of Islington,
The only man at a disguise in Middlesex.

Tub. But who shall write it?

Hilts. Scriben, the great writer. Scri. He'll do't alone, sir; he
will join with no man,
Though he be a joiner, in design he calls it,
He must be sole inventer. In-and-in
Draws with no other in's project, he will tell you,
It cannot else be feazible, or conduce:
Those are his ruling words; pleaze you to hear 'un?

Tub. Yes; master In-and-in, I have heard of you.

Med. I can do nothing, I.

Clench. He can do all, sir.

Med. They'll tell you so.

Tub. I'd have a toy presented,
A Tale of a Tub, a story of myself,
You can express a Tub?

Med. If it conduce
To the design, whate'er is *feasible:*
I can express a wash-house, if need be,
With a whole pedigree of Tubs.

Tub. No, one
Will be enough to note our name and family;
'Squire Tub of Totten, and to shew my adventures
This very day. I'd have it in Tub's Hall,
At Totten-Court, my lady mother's house;
My house indeed, for I am heir to it.

Med. If I might see the place, and had survey'd it,
I could say more: for all invention, sir,
Comes by degrees, and on the view of nature;
A world of things concur to the design.
Which makes it *feasible,* if art *conduce.*

Tub. You say well, witty master In-and-In.
How long have you studied ingine?

Med. Since I first
Join'd, or did in-lay in wit, some forty year.

Tub. A pretty time! — Basket, go you and wait
On master In-and-In to Totten-Court,
And all the other wise masters; shew them the hall,
And taste the language of the buttery to them.
Let them see all the tubs about the house,
That can raise matter, till I come — which shall be
Within an hour at least.

Clench. It will be glorious,
If In-and-In will undertake it, sir:
He has a monstrous Medlay-wit of his own.

Tub. Spare for no cost, either in boards or hoops,
To architect your tub: have you ne'er a cooper,
At London, call'd Vitruvius? send for him;
Or old John Heywood, call him to you, to help. Scri. He scorns
the motion, trust to him alone.
[Exeunt all but Tub.

Enter Lady TUB, *Dame* TURFE, CLAY, PUPPY, *and* WISPE.

Lady T. O, here's the 'squire! you slipp'd us finely, son.
These manners to your mother will commend you;
But in another age, not this: well, Tripoly,
Your father, good sir Peter, rest his bones,
Would not have done this; where's my huisher, Martin,
And your fair mistress Awdrey?

Tub. I not see them,
No creature but the four wise masters here,
Of Finsbury hundred, came to cry their constable,
Who, they do say, is lost.

Dame T. My husband lost,
And my fond daughter lost, I fear me too!
Where is your gentleman, madam? poor John Clay,
Thou has lost thy Awdrey.

Clay. I have lost my wits,
My little wits, good mother; I am distracted.

Pup. And I have lost my mistress, Dido Wispe,
Who frowns upon her Puppy, Hannibal.
Loss, loss on every side! a public loss!
Loss of my master! loss of his daughter! loss
Of favour, friends, my mistress! loss of all!

Enter TURFE and PREAMBLE.

Pre. What cry is this?

Turfe. My man speaks of some loss.

Pup. My master's found! good luck, an't be thy will,
Light on us all.

Dame T. O husband, are you alive!
They said you were lost.

Turfe. Where's justice Bramble's clerk?
Had he the money that I sent for?

Dame T. Yes,
Two hours ago, two fifty pounds in silver,
And Awdrey too.

Turfe. Why Awdrey? who sent for her?

Dame T. You, master Turfe, the fellow said.

Turfe. He lied.
I am cozen'd, robb'd, undone: your man's a thief,
And run away with my daughter, master Bramble,
And with my money.

Lady T. Neighbour Turfe, have patience;
I can assure you that your daughter's safe,
But for the monies, I know nothing of.

Turfe. My money is my daughter, and my daughter
She is my money, madam.

Pre. I do wonder
Your ladyship comes to know any thing
In these affairs.

Lady T. Yes, justice Preamble,
I met the maiden in the fields by chance,
In the 'squire's company, my son: how he
Lighted upon her, himself best can tell.

Tub. I intercepted her as coming hither,
To her father, who sent for her by Miles Metaphor,
Justice Preamble's clerk. And had your ladyship
Not hinder'd it, I had paid fine master justice
For his young warrant, and new pursuivant,
He serv'd it by this morning.

Pre. Know you that, sir?

Lady T. You told me, 'squire, a quite other tale,
But I believed you not; which made me send
Awdrey another way, by my Pol Martin,
And take my journey back to Kentish-town,
Where we found John Clay hidden in the barn,
To scape the hue and cry; and here he is.

Turfe. John Clay agen! nay, then — set cock-a-hoop:
I have lost no daughter, nor no money, justice.
John Clay shall pay; I'll look to you now, John.
Vaith, out it must, as good at night as morning.
I am e'en as vull as a piper's bag with joy,
Or a great gun upon carnation-day.
I could weep lions' tears to see you, John:
'Tis but two vifty pounds I have ventured for you,
But now I have you, you shall pay whole hundred.
Bun from your burroughs, son! faith, e'en be hang'd.
An you once earth yourself, John, in the barn,
I have no daughter vor you: who did verret 'un?

Dame T. My lady's son, the 'squire here, vetch'd 'un out.
Puppy had put us all in such a vright,
We thought the devil was in the barn; and nobody
Durst venture on 'un.

Turfe. I am now resolv'd
Who shall have my daughter.

Dame T. Who?

Turfe. He best deserves her.
Here comes the vicar. —

Enter Sir HUGH.

Canon Hugh, we have vound
John Clay agen! the matter's all come round.

Hugh. Is Metaphor return'd yet? *[Aside to Pre.*

Pre. All is turn'd
Here to confusion, we have lost our plot;
I fear my man is run away with the money,
And Clay is found, in whom old Turfe is sure
To save his stake.

Hugh. What shall we do then, justice?

Pre. The bride was met in the young 'squire's hands.

Hugh. And what's become of her?

Pre. None here can tell.

Tub. Was not my mother's man, Pol Martin, with you,
And a strange gentlewoman in his company,
Of late here, canon?

Hugh. Yes, and I dispatch'd them.

Tub. Dispatch'd them! how do you mean?

Hugh. Why, married them,
As they desired, but now.

Tub. And do you know
What you have done, sir Hugh?

Hugh. No harm, I hope.

Tub. You have ended all the quarrel: Awdrey is married.

Lady T. Married! to whom?

Turfe. My daughter Awdrey married,
And she not know of it!

Dame T. Nor her father or mother!

Lady T. Whom hath she married?

Tub. Your Pol Martin, madam;
A groom was never dreamt of.

Turfe. Is he a man?

Lady T. That he is, Turfe, and a gentleman I have made him.

Dame T. Nay, an he be a gentleman, let her shift.

Hugh. She was so brave, I knew her not, I swear;
And yet I married her by her own name:
But she was so disguised, so lady-like,
I think she did not know herself the while!
I married them as a mere pair of strangers,
And they gave out themselves for such.

Lady T. I wish them
Much joy, as they have given me heart's ease.

Tub. Then, madam, I'll entreat you now remit
Your jealousy of me; and please to take
All this good company home with you to supper:
We'll have a merry night of it, and laugh.

Lady T. A right good motion, 'squire, which I yield to;
And thank them to accept it. — Neighbour Turfe,
I'll have you merry, and your wife; and you,
Sir Hugh, be pardon'd this your happy error,
By justice Preamble, your friend and patron.

Pre. If the young 'squire can pardon it, I do.
[Exeunt all but Puppy, Wispe, and Hugh.

Pup. Stay, my dear Dido; and, good vicar Hugh,
We have a business with you; in short, this:
If you dare knit another pair of strangers,
Dido of Carthage, and her countryman,
Stout Hannibal stands to't. I have ask'd consent,
And she hath granted.

Hugh. But saith Dido so?

Wispe. Prom what Ball Hanny hath said, I dare not go.

Hugh. Come in then, I'll dispatch you: a good supper
Would not be lost, good company, good discourse;
But above all, where wit hath any source. *[Exeunt.*

SCENE III

TOTTEN-COURT. — Before the House.

Enter POL MARTIN, AWDREY, TUB, Lady TUB, PREAMBLE TURFE, Dame TURFE, and CLAY.

Pol. After the hoping of your pardon, madam,
For many faults committed, here my wife
And I do stand expecting your mild doom.

Lady T. I wish thee joy, Pol Martin, and thy wife
As much, mistress Pol Martin. Thou hast trick'd her
Up very fine, methinks.

Pol. For that I made
Bold with your ladyship's wardrobe, but have trespass'd
Within the limits of your leave — I hope.

Lady T. I give her what she wears; I know all women
Love to be fine: thou hast deserv'd it of me;
I am extremely pleased with thy good fortune.
Welcome, good justice Preamble; and, Turfe,
Look merrily on your daughter: she has married
A gentleman.

Turfe. So methinks. I dare not touch her,
She is so fine; yet I will say, God bless her!

Dame T. And I too, my fine daughter! could love her
Now twice as well as if Clay had her.

Tub. Come, come, my mother is pleased; I pardon all:
Pol Martin, in and wait upon my lady.
Welcome, good guests! see supper be serv'd in,
With all the plenty of the house and worship.
I must confer with master In-and-In
About some alterations in my masque:
Send Hilts out to me; bid him bring the council
Of Finsbury hither. *[Exeunt all but Tub.]* I'll have such a night
Shall make the name of Totten-Court immortal,
And be recorded to posterity. —

Enter MEDLAY, CLENCH, PAN, and SCRIBEN.

O master In-and-In! what have you done?

Med. Survey'd the place, sir, and design'd the ground,
Or stand-still of the work: and this it is.
First, I have fixed in the earth a tub,
And an old tub, like a salt-petre tub,
Preluding by your father's name, sir Peter,
And the antiquity of your house and family,
Original from salt-petre.

Tub. Good, i'faith,
You have shewn reading and antiquity here, sir.

Med. I have a little knowledge in design,
Which I can vary, sir, to *infinito*.

Tub. Ad infinitum, sir, you mean.

Med. I do,
I stand not on my Latin; I'll invent,
But I must be alone then, join'd with no man:
This we do call the stand-still of our work.

Tub. Who are those We you now join'd to yourself?

Med. I mean myself still in the plural number.
And out of this we raise Our Tale of a Tub.

Tub. No, master In-and-In, My Tale of a Tub,
By your leave; I am Tub, the Tale's of me,
And my adventures! I am 'squire Tub,
Subjectum fabulce.

Med. But I the author.

Tub. The workman, sir, the artificer; I grant you.
So Skelton-laureat was of Elinour Rumming,
But she the subject of the rout and tunning.

Clench. He has put you to it, neighbour In-and-In.

Pan. Do not dispute with him; he still will win
That pays for all. Scri. Are you revised o' that?
A man may have wit, and yet put off his hat.

Med. Now, sir, this Tub I will have capt with paper,
A fine oil'd lanthorn paper that we use.

Pan. Yes, every barber, every cutler has it.

Med. Which in it doth contain the light to the business;
And shall with the very vapour of the candle
Drive all the motions of our matter about,
As we present them. For example, first,
The worshipful lady Tub —

Tub. Right worshipful,
I pray you, I am worshipful myself.

Med. Your 'squireship's mother passeth by (her huisher,
Master Pol Martin, bare-headed before her)
In her velvet gown.

Tub. But how shall the spectators,
As it might be I, or Hilts, know 'tis my mother,
Or that Pol Martin, there, that walks before her?

Med. O we do nothing, if we clear not that.

Clench. You have seen none of his works, sir!

Pan. All the postures
Of the trained bands of the country. *Scri.* All their colours.

Pan. And all their captains.

Clench. All the cries of the city,
And all the trades in their habits. *Scri.* He has
His whistle of command, seat of authority,
And virge to interpret, tipt with silver, sir;
You know not him.

Tub. Well, I will leave all to him.

Med. Give me the brief of your subject. Leave the whole
State of the thing to me.

Enter HILTS.

Hilts. Supper is ready, sir,
My lady calls for you.

Tub. I'll send it you in writing.

Med. Sir, I will render *feasible* and facile
What you expect.

Tub. Hilts, be it your care,
To see the wise of Finsbury made welcome:
Let them want nothing. Is old Rosin sent for?

Hilts. He's come within. *[Exit Tub.* Scri. Lord, what a world of business
The 'squire dispatches!

Med. He's a learned man:
I think there are but vew o' the inns of court,
Or the inns of chancery like him.

Clench. Care to fit 'un then. *[Exeunt.*

SCENE IV

The same. — A Room in the House.

Enter Black Jack and HILTS.

Jack. Yonder's another wedding, master Basket,
Brought in by vicar Hugh.

Hilts. What are they, Jack?

Jack. The high constable's man, Ball Hanny, and mistress Wispe,
Our lady's woman.

Hilts. And are the table merry?

Jack. There's a young tilemaker makes 'em all laugh;
He will not eat his meat, but cries at the board,
He shall be hang'd.

Hilts. He has lost his wench already:
As good be hang'd.

Jack. Was she that is Pol Martin,
Our fellow's mistress, wench to that sneak-John?

Hilts. I'faith, Black Jack, he should have been her bridegroom:
But I must go to wait on my wise masters.
Jack, you shall wait on me, and see the masque anon;
I am half lord chamberlain in my master's absence.

Jack. Shall we have a masque? who makes it?

Hilts. In-and-In,
The maker of Islington: come, go with me
To the sage sentences of Finsbury. *[Exeunt.*

SCENE V

Another Room in the same, with a curtain drawn across it.

Enter Tub, followed by two Grooms, with chairs, etc., and ROSIN and his two Boys.

1 Groom. Come, give us in the great chair for my lady,
And set it there; and this for justice Bramble.

2 Groom. This for the 'squire my master, on the right hand.

1 Groom. And this for the high constable.

2 Groom. This his wife.

1 Groom. Then for the bride and bridegroom here, Pol Martin.

2 Groom. And she Pol Martin at my lady's feet.

1 Groom. Right.

2 Groom. And beside them master Hannibal Puppy.

1 Groom. And his She-Puppy, mistress Wispe that was:
Here's all are in the note.

2 Groom. No, master vicar;
The petty canon Hugh.
1 Groom. And cast-by Clay:
There they are all.

Tub. Then cry a hall! a hall!
'Tis merry in Tottenham-hall, when beards wag all:
Come, father Rosin, with your fiddle now,
And two tall toters; flourish to the masque. *[Loud music.*

Enter PREAMBLE-, Lady TUB, TURFE, Dame TURFE, POL MARTIN AWDREY, PUPPY, WISPE, HUGH, CLAY; all take their seats.

HILTS *waits on the by.*

Lady T. Neighbours all, welcome! Now doth Totten-hall
Shew like a court: and hence shall first be call'd so.
Your witty short confession, master vicar,
Within, hath been the prologue, and hath open'd
Much to my son's device, his Tale of a Tub.

Tub. Let my masque shew itself, and In-and-In,
The architect, appear: I hear the whistle.

Hilts. Peace!

MEDLAY *appears above the curtain.*

Med. Thus rise I first in my light linen breeches,
To run the meaning over in short speeches.
Here is a Tub, a Tub of Totten-Court,
An ancient Tub has call'd you to this sport:
His father was a knight, the rich sir Peter,
Who got his wealth by a Tub, and by salt-petre;
And left all to his lady Tub, the mother
Of this bold 'squire Tub, and to no other.
Now of this Tub and's deeds, not done in ale,
Observe, and you shall see the very Tale.
[He draws the curtain, and discovers the top of the Tnb.

THE FIRST MOTION.

Med. Here canon Hugh first brings to Totten-hall
The high constable's council, tells the 'squire all;
Which, though discover'd, give the devil his due,
The wise of Finsbury do still pursue.
Then with the justice doth he counterplot,
And his clerk Metaphor, to cut that knot;
Whilst lady Tub, in her sad velvet gown,
Missing her son, doth seek him up and down.

Tub. With her Pol Martin bare before her.

Med. Yes,
I have exprest it here in figure, and Mistress Wispe, her
woman, holding up her train.

Tub. In the next page report your second strain.

THE SECOND MOTION.

Med. Here the high constable and sages walk
To church: the dame, the daughter, bride-maids talk
Of wedding-business; till a fellow in comes,
Relates the robbery of one captain Thums:
Chargeth the bridegroom with it, troubles all,
And gets the bride; who in the hands doth fall
Of the bold 'squire; but thence soon is ta'en
By the sly justice and his clerk profane,
In shape of pursuivant; which he not long
Holds, but betrays all with his trembling tongue:
As truth will break out and shew —

Tub. O thou hast made him kneel there in a corner,
I see now: there's a simple honour for you, Hilts!

Hilts. Did I not make him to confess all to you?

Tub. True, In-and-In hath done you right, you see —
Thy third, I pray thee, witty In-and-In.

Clench. The 'squire commends'un; he doth like all well.

Pan. He cannot choose: this is gear made to sell.

THE THIRD MOTION.

Med. The careful constable here drooping comes
In his deluded search of captain Thums.
Puppy brings word his daughter's run away
With the tall serving-man, he frights groom Clay
Out of his wits: Returneth then the 'squire,
Mocks all their pains, and gives fame out a liar,
For falsely charging Clay, when 'twas the plot
Of subtle Bramble, who had Awdrey got
Into his hand by this winding device.
The father makes a rescue in a trice:
And with his daughter, like St. George on foot,
Comes home triumphing to his dear heart-root,
And tells the lady Tub, whom he meets there,
Of her son's courtesies, the batchelor,
Whose words had made 'em fait the hue and cry.
When captain Thums coming to ask him, why
He had so done; he cannot yield him cause:
But so he runs his neck into the laws.

THE FOURTH MOTION.

Med. The laws, who have a noose to crack his neck,
   A s justice Bramble tells him, who doth peck
   A hundred pound out of his purse, that comes
   Like his teeth from him, unto captain Thums.
       Thums is the vicar in a false disguise;
       And employs Metaphor to fetch this prize.
       Who tells the secret unto Basket-Hilts,
       For fear of beating. This the' squire quilts
       Within his cap; and bids him but purloin
   The wench for him; they two shall share the coin.
       Which the sage lady in her 'foresaid gown,
       Breaks off, returning unto Kentish-town,
       To seek her Wispe; taking the 'squire along,
   Who finds Clay John, as hidden in straw throng.

Hilts. O how am I beholden to the inventor,
   That would not, on record, against me enter,
       My slackness here to enter in the barn:
       Well, In-and-In, I see thou canst discern!

Tub. On with your last, and come to a conclusion.

THE FIFTH MOTION.

Med. The last is known, and needs but small infusion
       Into your memories, by leaving in
       These figures as you sit. I, In-and-In,
       Present you with the show: first, of a lady
   Tub, and her son, of whom this masque here made I.
       Then bridegroom Pol, and mistress Pol the bride,
       With the sub-couple, who sit them beside.

Tub. That only verse I alter'd for the better.
       Euphonia gratia.

Med. Then justice Bramble, with sir Hugh the canon:
And the bride's parents, which I will not stan' on,
Or the lost Clay, with the recovered Miles:
Who thus unto his master him reconciles.
On the 'squire's word, to pay old Turfe his club.
And so doth end our Tale here of a Tub. [Exeunt.

THE EPILOGUE

BY 'SQUIRE TUB.

This tale of me, the Tub of Totten-Court,
A poet first invented for your sport.
Wherein the fortune of most empty tubs,
Rolling in love, are shewn; and with what rubs
We are commonly encountered: when the wit
Of the whole hundred so opposeth it,
Our petty canon's forked plot in chief,
Sly justice' arts, with the high constable's brief
And brag commands; my lady mother's care,
And her Pol Martin's fortune; with the rare
Fate of poor John, thus tumbled in the cask;
Cot In-and-In to givg it you in a masque:
That you be pleased, who come to see a play,
With those that hear, and mark not what we say.
Wherein the poet's fortune is, I fear,
Still to be early up, but ne'er the near.

CPSIA information can be obtained
at www.ICGtesting.com
Printed in the USA
LVOW04s2010270616
494284LV00042B/1724/P